Developing a Counselor-in-Training Program for Camps

Jessica Furie
Eric Nicastro
Rachel Saslove

©2012 Healthy Learning. All rights reserved. Printed in the United States.

No part of this book may be reproduced, stored in a retrieval system, or transmitted, in any form or by any means, electronic, mechanical, photocopying, recording, or otherwise, without the prior permission of Healthy Learning. Throughout this book, the masculine shall be deemed to include the feminine and vice versa.

ISBN: 978-1-60679-209-4
Library of Congress Control Number: 2012932194
Cover design: Alexandra Furie
Book layout: Roger W. Rybkowski

Healthy Learning
P.O. Box 1828
Monterey, CA 93942
www.healthylearning.com

Dedication

To Max, for being a great life partner and always pushing me to do what makes me happy. To my parents, for deciding to send me to camp and believing in me. To Ally and Sam, camp never would have been the same without both of you. "Furies unite!"

—Jessica

To Doug Lynn, Louis Bordman, and every other camp supervisor I have ever had. Their training and passion for working with kids in a camp setting instilled in me the skills, the know-how, and the care it takes to change a kid's life through a camping experience. To my wife and great love Jessica, as well as my mother Alice, for being the best support system any one person could ask for.

—Eric

To Ron, KK, and Jeff, for the incredible opportunities and the infinite wisdom and guidance. To the CG CITs, for being my guinea pigs and success stories. To my friends, for the years of collaboration and encouragement, and unending patience for listening to all my camp stories. And of course, to my amazing crazy family who are my constant inspiration, endless supporters, and proof that you're never too old to go to camp!

—Rachel

Acknowledgments

We would like to acknowledge the following people for the help and support that they have given us throughout the process of creating this book. We would like to thank Todd Zinn, Hayley Dox, and Erica Feinman, who used the first version of this book when running their CIT programs. They each took the time to give us feedback on how to improve our curriculum. Andrew Benkendorf has been instrumental in creating a foundation to conceptualize homesickness and managing camper behavior. Andrew was a key figure in teaching Jessica how conceptualize psychological issues with in the context of camp. Andrew also helped to co-create Program #16: Setting Consequences. We would also like to acknowledge Lauren Viner, a fellow camp-lover and terrific educator, who not only served as a sounding board for Rachel throughout the development of this curriculum, but also co-created Program #2: The Good, the Bad, and the Ugly, Program #3: Red Light, Green Light, You're Fired! and Program #14: Guess Who? Lastly, we would like to thank Alexandra Furie, for creating the beautiful front cover to this book.

Contents

Dedication.. 3
Acknowledgments... 5
Introduction 8

Chapter 1: Guiding Your CIT Program
Developing Your Own Programs...................................... 9
Program #1: Expectations for You and Yours................... 11

Chapter 2: What Is a Camp Counselor?
Philosophy and Basic Concepts...................................... 13
Program #2: The Good, the Bad, and the Ugly................. 15
Program #3: Red Light, Green Light, You're Fired!............ 18

Chapter 3: Counseling Skills
Philosophy and Basic Concepts...................................... 22
Program #4: Introduction to Active Listening 25
Program #5: Ready, Set, Communicate! 27
Program #6: Communication Barriers 29
Program #7: Non-Verbal Communication 31
Program #8: Something to Talk About 33
Program #9: How Do You Feel?...................................... 36
Program #10: Guide to Assessing Camper Problems......... 38
Program #11: Introduction to Discussion Leading............. 39
Program #12: Practice Discussion Leading 41

Chapter 4: Knowing Your Campers
Philosophy and Basic Concepts...................................... 43
Program #13: Awks and Gawks...................................... 45
Program #14: Guess Who?.. 53
Program #15: The Other Side of the Tracks..................... 58

Chapter 5: Managing Camper Behavior
Philosophy and Basic Concepts... 60
Program #16: Setting Consequences... 65
Program #17: Bully for You 70
Program #18: Active Duty—Counseling Skill Role-Play 77
Program #19: Why Can't They Just Get Along?.................................. 83
Program #20: Conflict Escalation 92

Chapter 6: Working With Groups
Philosophy and Basic Concepts... 94
Program #21: Stages of Group Development 96
Program #22: Puzzled 99
Program #23: Group Dynamics—Meal Time Fun 101
Program #24: Cabin Dynamics... 104

Chapter 7: Leadership
Philosophy and Basic Concepts... 106
Program #25: You Can Lead the Way.. 107
Program #26: It's Just My Style 116
Program #27: When I Grow Up—Setting the Example 120
Program #28: Taking Responsibility 124

Chapter 8: Programming
Philosophy and Basic Concepts... 127
The Path and Process of Wow: Keys to Writing a Successful Program 128
Seven Main Program Vehicles 131

About the Authors... 133

Introduction

This book was created after Jessica's experience as a counselor-in-training director. As the leader of this program, she searched the Internet for books about content for a counselor-in-training programs. After finding no such literature, she decided to create her own curriculum. The story was the same for Rachel and Eric, who have both run counselor-in-training programs for many years. This curriculum is the "greatest hits" of all of their programs. Each program in this curriculum has been run by various individuals many of times. Careful feedback has been given about each program, and adaptations have been made to make the book as user-friendly as possible.

This book is structured in a way that allows the counselor-in-training director to use 28 ready-made programs, or create his own programs. Chapter 1 introduces different program structures that the CIT director can use as a vehicle to deliver different content. The subsequent chapters start with a core concepts section that introduces different concepts that can be pulled, if the director wants to create his own programs. For example, when Jessica was creating her CIT program, she wanted to know what specific camper issues she should teach. The director who uses this book can open Chapter 5: Managing Camper Behavior and read a quick blurb under Philosophy and Basic Concepts about homesickness, cutting, bullying, death, divorce, and so forth. Following Philosophy and Basic Concepts, each chapter contains programs that we have created. So if the director does not want to create his own program about bullying, he can use the ready-made program. The figures referenced in any given program can be found at the end of that program.

Although this book can be adapted for general staff training, the CIT summer is a unique experience, and this book touches on that transition.

1

Guiding Your CIT Program

Developing Your Own Programs

The art of creating strong programs is identifying the core concepts that you want to teach. Once the goals are established, many vehicles are available from which to choose to help you accomplish your goal. Some common vehicles of program delivery are as follows:

Debate: CITs split into groups to support a certain view, side, or decision.

Direct camper interaction: CITs observe or participate in an activity with the campers and later debrief the experience.

Discussion-based program: A leader poses a series of questions that help guide conversation. This program can be lead by CIT directors, other staff members, or peers.

Didactic: This approach can be a traditional lecture. This method is often used in conjunction with other methods, such as role-plays or simulations.

Experiential: CITs engage in a real-life experience that is used as a base to understand and learn about concepts. This method can include team-building or ropes course games.

Fish bowl: Some participants sit on the inside of the circle, while others sit on the outside. The outside members ask the inside members questions, or the facilitator can ask the inside members questions while the others watch.

Games: This method incorporates the use of points or competition, which can be something such as teaching material by playing *Family Feud,* or even just giving points for a correct answer.

Observation: CITs will observe a certain part of the day or a certain activity.

Panel: A group of staff or counselors that answers questions or discusses a certain topic.

Performance: Members prepare something to show in front of the group.

Reflective/alone time: CITs will be asked to take some time by themselves to explore a prompt before returning to the group.

Role-plays: Acting-out scenarios are very effective for teaching counseling skills. The many variations of role-playing include: demonstration (CIT leaders model a certain skill in front of the group), small groups role-play, two or three members role-play in front of the group, or use of station rotation in role-play. (CITs rotate through different spaces, where they engage in different role-plays on the same topic of various topics). Role-play topics can be chosen by CIT director or by the CITs. CITs can write down topics they have faced or that they are worried about on note cards, and these note cards can be used as prompts.

Small group work: CITs will split into groups to complete a parallel task and share their experience/product, or CITs will engage in different tasks and share their knowledge.

Station rotation: Multiple topics are presented at different locations or in different parts of a room. The group is split up into subgroups and travel through each of the stations.

Use of space to explore decision-making: Explore decision-making by preparing prompts and designating different parts of a room for different answers. For example, one corner of a room is agree, one is disagree, and one is unsure. After a prompt is asked, CITs will go to the corner that supports their thinking. This end can also be conducted CITs by crossing over a chalk-drawn line if they agree/disagree.

Program #1: Expectations for You and Yours

Note: This section can be used to help set the frame for your CIT summer.

Goals:
- To help CITs understand what everyone on the senior staff expects of them
- To help CITs understand how the daily schedule impacts their day and how they can be impactful during each moment of the day
- To help CITs understand that the expectations of others can impact their work positively and negatively

Timed Procedure:

0:00 – 0:05	Introduction
0:05 – 0:25	Daily schedule activity
0:25 – 0:35	Discussion
0:35 – 0:55	Expectations activity
0:55 – 0:60	Wrap-up

DETAILED PROCEDURE

00:00 – 00:05: Introduction

The group leader will begin by discussing the difference between the day of a senior staff member, the day of the camper, and the day of a staff member. The group leader will talk about the differences in the roles each one plays.

00:05 – 00:25: Daily Schedule Activity

Each CIT will be given a sample of a daily schedule at camp. This sample will provide space for the CITs to write about what they feel they should be doing during each hour of the day. The CITs will then be split into small groups and share what they wrote.

00:25 – 00:35: Discussion

The group leader will ask the CITs to share answers with the entire group. The group will then discuss why they do the things they do as the day progresses and how what they, do helps keep camp moving in a successful direction.

00:35 – 00:55: Expectations Activity

Each position at camp will be written on butcher paper and put onto tables. The group leader will then have time to go around and write the expectations they have for each of these positions for the summer. Discussion will go around the room, and each list of expectations will be read out loud.

00:55 – 00:60: Wrap-Up

The group leader will go over how expectations can have positive and negative impacts on what they do and how it is important to be mindful throughout the summer of the expectations counselors have for themselves and the expectations others have of them.

2

What Is a Camp Counselor?

Philosophy and Basic Concepts

The Scarecrow Versus the Tin Man

Which type of counselor is best? Is it the counselor who uses feeling and thought when making decisions? Or is it the counselor who takes his time and thinks through the decisions he makes? On the other hand it might be both. Doesn't the counselor who works with campers using heart and feeling merit the respect of being called a good, caring counselor? As well as the counselor who makes the best decisions for his campers because he weighs the pros and the cons of the actions he is about take. Which counselor should be working with kids?

The counselor who shows heart and passion above all else can oftentimes be called the "Scarecrow." Being this counselor is beneficial because campers need a nurturing, caring figure during their camp experience. This counselor will often be there emotionally for the campers and go out of his way to make them feel good. However, this approach can often result in bad decision-making. Many of these Scarecrow counselors end up making decisions rashly or getting easily overwhelmed when something doesn't go their way. Why can this happen? The issue with an emotional counselor is that he can easily forget to critically analyze a situation, and thus, emotions may hinder the counselor from thinking of alternative options. An emotional counselor can also be subject to allowing personal issues to get in the way of taking care of his campers.

The "Tin Man," however, does not have the issue of getting too emotional. Instead the Tin Man counselor can be insensitive to campers because he spends too much time thinking about the decisions. This approach can lead to decisions that make sense in terms of safety and the well-being of the camper, but what happens to a counselor who doesn't put the emotion and heart in the work they do? It is easy for a camper to tell when a counselor doesn't really care about him. This situation can leave a stain on the camper's experience as the love of the counselors means the world to him. It is essential to make smart and calculated decisions at camp, but heart and passion is what helps change campers' lives.

No winner emerges between these two counselors. The ideal is to really be both. You must have passion, heart, and soul in everything you do when working with kids and have the ability to think through each decision you make carefully. Being perfect is not a possibility in the camping world, but being great is. Campers feed off of your passion and thrive in the good decisions you make about their experience. To be a great counselor, you have to see "Oz" and make sure you have the heart and the brain.

Basic Concepts

Cabin Counselor Versus a Camp Counselor

A cabin counselor is a counselor who looks only after his own cabin. He does his job, fulfilling the letter of the law rather than the spirit of the law. A camp counselor is one who helps promote a high level of energy at the camp, connect with campers outside his cabin, and someone who works to better the greater good of camp.

Boundaries

Boundaries is a concept that should be revisited throughout the summer. What is the line between being a friend and being a counselor? What are the camp rules? Should CITs carry campers, hold their hands, or let them sit on their laps? What message does this send to that specific camper and to the rest of the cabin? Although the rule to not let camper's sit on counselors' laps may be a clear rule, most decisions that CITs make will have no right or wrong answer. Dialogue about these issues is the best way to help guide the CITs in developing healthy boundaries.

Qualities of a Camp Counselor

It can be helpful to help distinguish the good qualities of a camp counselor. By thinking back about counselors in the past, observing current counselors and reflecting on what they did well, or imagining what traits would make us the best counselor, counselors can design a counselor "superhero" and decide what traits he will have.

Program #2: The Good, the Bad, and the Ugly

Goals:
- To help CITs differentiate the qualities of a good staff member and the qualities of a bad staff member
- To provide the CITs an opportunity to share experiences they've had with staff members, and what made those experiences good
- To give the CITs a chance to voice opinions on what they think it means to be a good staff member

Materials:
- Large floor space
- GBU and Q cards
- Chart paper with definitions of Good, Bad, and Ugly
- Paper
- Pencils

Material Preparation:
To create GBU cards, write "good," "bad," and "ugly," on 12 index cards each, for a total of 36 GBU cards. To create Q cards, write the good, bad, and ugly qualities listed under the detailed procedure onto index cards, for a total of 30 Q cards.

Timed Procedure:
0:00 – 0:10   Settle in and mini-discussion
0:10 – 0:15   Explanation of the game
0:15 – 0:45   The Good, the Bad, and the Ugly
0:45 – 1:05   Discussion
1:05 – 1:10   Wrap-up

DETAILED PROCEDURE

0:00 – 0:10: Settle in and Mini-Discussion

The facilitator will pose the following questions to the CITs:
- Is there such thing as an ideal counselor?
- What does that person look like?
- What is the most important quality a good counselor must have?

0:10 – 0:15: Explanation of the Game

Note: GBU = Good/Bad/Ugly card; Q = Quality card

The facilitator will separate the CITs into four groups in order to play a large game of memory using the GBU and Q cards. The cards should all be placed upside-down and spread out on a flat surface. Each team will take turns flipping over cards, looking for a match. At the end of the game, the points are tallied to see which team wins. A correct match results in a point being added to the team's score. An incorrect match results in a point being taken away from the team's score. The facilitator will remind the teams that incorrect matches result in losing points. The cards should be spread out on the floor (laid out neatly, but not in order). The facilitator will instruct the CITs to flip over two cards at a time. If two GBU cards are flipped over, their turn is over. If two Q cards are flipped over, their turn is over. If, however, a GBU card and a Q card are flipped over, the CITs have two choices:

- They decide the quality matches with the description (good/bad/ugly) and keep the pair of cards, receiving another turn. They will keep getting turns as long as they make matches on the first flip.
- They flip over a GBU card and a Q card and decide that the quality doesn't match the description (good/bad/ugly). They can turn their GBU card back over, and flip over another card with the hopes of finding a second GBU card. If they flip over another Q card, their turn is over. If they flip over a GBU card, they must then decide whether or not they believe it matches the quality they've already found. If they believe it matches their card, they can keep the cards, but their turn is over. If they decide it doesn't match, they turn both cards back over and their turn is over.

Good is defined as something that is an obviously good quality to have as a staff member. Bad is defined as a quality that is wrong to possess within a camp environment, and Ugly is defined as something that is inappropriate for both camp and in life.

Good Qualities (12)

- Supportive
- Fair
- Punctual
- Good listener
- Leads the person to the answer without giving advice
- Always enthused
- Takes everyone/everything into account
- Inclusive
- Responsible
- Caring
- Ensures camper safety
- Prioritizes

Bad Qualities (8)

- Skips programs
- Comes back late from days/periods off

- Stays out past curfew
- Easily angered
- Narrow-minded
- Apathetic
- Uninvolved
- Gossips about co-counselors

Ugly Qualities (10)

- Comes on to campers
- Has no boundaries
- Never sleeps
- Breaks rules
- Disrespectful
- Gossips with campers
- Exclusive
- Physically aggressive
- Ignores campers
- Plays favorites

0:15 – 0:45: The Good, the Bad, and the Ugly

Play the game. When all the qualities have been matched up, the facilitator will tally the score.

0:45 – 1:05: Discussion

The facilitator will ask the CITs if they have any qualities that they feel are missing from the list. The goal is to have a comprehensive list of qualities of a good staff member. Possible discussion questions include:
- What are things a counselor should avoid when trying to be a good staff member, and why?
- What are things that make people stand out as good or bad staff to their supervisor? What about to their kids?
- What is the point of even trying?
- What kind of impact does having good/bad staff have on a camper's summer?
- Do the campers notice when their staff are doing a bad job?

1:05 – 1:10: Wrap-Up

Program #3: Red Light, Green Light, You're Fired!

Goals:
- To help CITs understand and appreciate the importance of boundaries at camp
- To provide clarity about some of the things that take place at camp and whether or not they are allowed

Materials:
- Large floor space
- Pack of prepared cue cards (18 scenario cards and 28 result cards, divided into green, red, yellow, and you're fired cards)
- Piece of paper to tally points

Material Preparation:
Paste the 18 scenarios from Figure 2-1 onto index cards to create scenario cards. Also create seven index cards with the word *yellow,* seven with the word *green,* seven with the word *red,* and seven with the phrase *you're fired.*

Timed Procedure:
0:00 – 0:05 Explanation
0:05 – 0:45 Play Green Light, Red Light
0:45 – 1:00 Discussion

DETAILED PROCEDURE

0:00 – 0:05: Explanation

Separate your group into two teams. The teams take turns flipping over cards, looking for a match. At the end of the game, points are tallied to see which team wins. A correct match results in a point being added to the team's score. An incorrect match results in a point being taken away from the team's score. Please remind your teams that incorrect matches result in losing points.

0:05 – 0:45: Play Green Light, Red Light

Instructions for the Game

Spread the cards out on the floor, jumbled (not in order). Instruct the first group of CITs to flip over two cards and see if they match. Different things happen based on which cards are flipped over. (For the purpose of this outline, A = action and R = result.) If they flip over:
- A and A = no turn
- R and R = no turn

- A and R = two options
    - ✓ Option 1: The CITs flip over a results card and an action card and decide that the two are a match, they keep the pair, and they then get another turn, knowing that an incorrect match will mean a point taken away at the end of the game.
    - ✓ Option 2: The CITs flip over a results card and an action card and decide that the two are not a match. They can put back their results card and flip another card with the hopes of finding a second results card. If they flip over another action card, their turn is over. If they flip over a results card, they must then decide whether or not they believe it matches their action card. If they decide it does match, they keep the cards, but their turn is over. If they decide it doesn't match, they turn the cards back over, and their turn is over.

Results

Green light = Thumbs up! 100 percent okay.
Yellow light = Be cautious/use your own judgment.
Red light   = You probably shouldn't do it, but you probably won't get fired for doing it. Action will probably warrant a warning.
You're fired = 100 percent not okay, even if you don't get caught.

- Green Light
    - ✓ Sammy, a 12-year-old boy, got up on skis for the first time, and his staff gives him a congratulatory hug.
    - ✓ You and your significant other sit together during a camp activity.
    - ✓ Your 11-year-old campers are having trouble falling asleep. They come and sit on your bed while you tell them a story.
    - ✓ 14-year-old Rebecca comes to you with a personal issue. You share the problem with your co-staff.
- Yellow Light
    - ✓ Your 10-year-old campers are asking you about their sexuality. You and your co-staff address the issues with your campers.
    - ✓ You become involved in a sexual relationship with your supervisor.
    - ✓ You come back late from your day off.
    - ✓ You let your 14-year-old boys sneak out after lights out to the girl's village.
- Red Light
    - ✓ Your boyfriend/girlfriend comes to camp to visit on your day off. You give him/her a tour of camp and bring him/her into your cabin.
    - ✓ Your 11-year-old camper, Jessie, is extremely homesick. You lend her your cell phone to call home.
    - ✓ You are having a water fight with your campers at the lake. One of them doesn't want to participate, but you throw him into the lake anyway.

- ✓ You are a staff member for 12-year-olds, and you and your fellow co-staff rotate the wake-up song in the morning. This week, it's "Your Love is My Drug." Last week, it was "Apple Bottom Jeans, Boots With the Fur." Can't wait for next week!
  - ✓ You are a junior male counselor, and a 13-year-old girl wants to sit in your lap at every program.
- You're Fired
  - ✓ You're really feeling the burn after a hard day's work. You and your friends take a shot of vodka during rest hour.
  - ✓ You have signed out for your day off, and you are getting water at the spring for the drive to town. You light a joint at the end of the gate.
  - ✓ It's Color War, and you and your co-CIT captain are closing up Arts and Crafts for the night. You make out.
  - ✓ You are horsing around with your kids in the pool. One of them gives you a purple nurple. You return the favor by giving them a five star.
  - ✓ You come back from your day off drunk.

0:45 – 1:00 Discussion

Suggested Questions

- Were there any actions that you disagreed with? If so, which ones and why?
- For the yellow light (and even some of the red light) actions that you are unsure about, ask yourself these questions before coming to your supervisor:
  - ✓ Is the action going against camp rules?
  - ✓ If you do the action, will everyone in your cabin be comfortable? Will everyone be safe?
  - ✓ What might be a consequence for doing the action?
  - ✓ Are you still not sure? Ask your supervisor.

Sammy, a 12-year-old boy, got up on skis for the first time, and his staff gives him a congratulatory hug.	You're really feeling the burn after a hard day's work. You and your friends take a shot of vodka during rest hour.
You and your significant other sit together during a camp activity.	You have signed out for your day off, and you are getting water at the spring for the drive to town. You light a joint at the end of the gate.
Your 11-year-old campers are having trouble falling asleep. They come and sit on your bed while you tell them a story.	It's Color War, and you and your co-CIT captain are closing up Arts and Crafts for the night. You make out.
14-year-old Rebecca comes to you with a personal issue. You share the problem with your co-staff.	You are horsing around with your kids in the pool. One of them gives you a purple nurple. You return the favor by giving them a five star.
Your boyfriend/girlfriend comes to camp to visit on your day off. You give him/her a tour of camp and bring him/her into your cabin.	You come back from your day off drunk.
Your 10-year-old campers are asking you about their sexuality. You and your co-staff address the issues with your campers.	You are a junior male counselor, and a 13-year-old girl wants to sit in your lap at every program.
Your 11-year-old camper, Jessie, is extremely homesick. You lend her your cell phone to call home.	You are a staff member for 12-year-olds, and you and your fellow co-staff rotate the wake-up song in the morning. This week, it's "Your Love is My Drug." Last week it was "Apple Bottom Jeans, Boots With the Fur." Can't wait for next week!
You become involved in a sexual relationship with your supervisor.	You are having a water fight with your campers at the lake. One of them doesn't want to participate, but you throw him into the lake anyway.
You let your 14-year-old boys sneak out after lights out to the girls' village.	You come back late from your day off.

Figure 2-1. Red Light, Green Light, You're Fired scenarios

3

Counseling Skills

Philosophy and Basic Concepts

When most people think of basic counseling skills, they think of active listening. Active listening is a set of communication steps that include: encouraging others, clarifying statements, restating what the other person said, reflecting with feeling, summarizing the others statements, and validating concerns. Although these six skills are incredibly useful, most facilitators try to teach all six at one time. When this approach is attempted, the skills get lost and confused with one another. Therefore, you should either break down the skills and teach them on different days, or teach the two that are most important: identifying non-verbal behavior and reflecting feeling.

Basic Concepts

Non-Verbal Behavior

Non-verbal behavior includes eye contact, facial expressions, body language and posture, mirroring, and proximity.
- Eye contact: Eye contact conveys attention. However, don't stare into the other person's eyes. Some suggest intervals of four to five seconds of eye contact.
- Body language and posture: Lean slightly forward to show interest. Do not cross arms over chest.
- Mirroring: Match your body posture to that of the other person to whom you are talking, as if they were looking at themselves in the mirror. This technique conveys empathy.
- Proximity: Give someone enough space to feel comfortable. Angle your body toward the person to whom you are speaking. Do not sit directly facing each other.

Reflection of Feeling

This skill is key because this is how a camper feels understood. If the counselor can directly identify how someone is feeling (by using a "feeling word"), all of the other skills will fall into place. Even if a counselor cannot correctly identify the camper's feeling, but opens up a dialogue, the camper will feel safe to discuss how he is feeling. An example of this is, "You look like you are feeling sad."

Roadblocks

Although not a specific skill, it is often easier to learn what not to do. Roadblocks include: interrupting, knowing what is right, directing/ordering, threatening, always advising, and bypassing hard conversations.

Additional Skills

Many other skills not outlined in this book can be taught and integrated into the CIT program. These include: tone, rate of speech, validating statements, summarizing statements, I-statements, open-ended questions, exception questions, miracle questions, and scaling questions.

I-Statements

I-statements are useful to help people speak only for themselves, to help identify feelings, and to make a request about how they would like to be treated.

    I feel _____ when you _____ because_____.
        (feeling word)   (specific behavior)

    I would like _____.
         (state request)

Summarizing

The summarizing skill highlights key aspects of the discussion and sums it up at the end of the conversation. It helps make connections between relevant aspects of lengthy messages.

    *It seems to me what you are saying is*_____.

Exception Question

The camper will *always* have times when the problem is less severe or absent. The counselor seeks to encourage the camper to describe circumstances in which the problem does not show up. For example:
- *When are you not feeling homesick?*
- *When do you feel included in the cabin?*
- *What part of the day do you enjoy at camp?*

Miracle Question

The miracle question is great in helping campers see what their ideal situation would be. This technique is especially helpful when you ask campers what would make them feel better or less homesick and they tell you that they don't know. (For more information, refer to *Keys to Solutions in Brief Therapy* by Steve de Shazer [1985].)

The miracle question is: *If a miracle happened while you were asleep, and all of your problems were solved, what would it look like when you woke up?*

Scaling Questions

Ask the camper to rate where they fall on a scale of 1 to 10 about a specific issue. This skill helps determine how severe the problem is to the camper.

On a scale of 1 to 10—10 being this is the best day of your life, and 1 being the worse day of your life—how are you feeling today?

Program #4: Introduction to Active Listening

Goals:
- To introduce the concept of active listening
- To explore how important questions and listening are when you cannot make eye contact

Materials:
- Markers and paper

Timed Procedure:
0:00 – 0:15   Active listening simulation
0:15 – 0:30   Debrief the exercise

DETAILED PROCEDURE

0:00 – 0:15: Active Listening Simulation

Instruct CITs to find a partner and decide who is partner A and who is partner B. Partner A will draw a picture of his house. Partner B will be given the instructions to replicate partner A's drawings. Partner B is able to look at Partner A's picture and is allowed to ask questions. The pictures should then be shared with the group to show how similar or different the pictures are.

In the second round, Partner B will create a drawing that partner A must replicate. However, the second round, the partners are not able to look at each others' work. The must communicate their vision verbally while sitting back to back. Partner A is able to ask partner B questions. After this action is completed, the partner can compare drawings.

Variation: TINKERTOY®/LEGO® Simulation

Partner A will build something out of a TINKERTOY set or LEGO bricks. Partner B will replicate A's structure. Halfway through, partners should switch; however, this time, partner A must sit back-to-back with partner B, and is not able to look at the construction or structure. (Make sure each partner has a matching set of blocks or toys).

0:15 – 0:30: Debrief the Exercise

Engage in a dialogue about the task.

- What was different about the two rounds?
- What helped you complete the task?
- What were effective ways to communicate your ideas?
- What were barriers?

- What components are involved in "real" listening? (Construct a list with things such as eye contact, nodding head, responding, etc.)
- How often do people really suspend their thoughts to listen to what someone else has to say?

Program #5: Ready, Set, Communicate!

Goals:
- To emphasize how important communication is within a team and to help CITs improve upon their communication skills
- To allow CITs to participate in several challenges, testing their communication abilities
- To help CITs understand the frustration of poor communication so that they may not practice poor communication themselves

Materials:
- Large pack of LEGO bricks
- Several packs of markers
- Coloring book pages
- Paper
- Pencils

Timed Procedure:
0:00 – 0:05   Introduction
0:05 – 0:30   LEGO land
0:30 – 0:40   Charades
0:40 – 1:05   Coloring book
1:05 – 1:15   Wrap-up

DETAILED PROCEDURE

0:00 – 0:05: Introduction

The CITs will grab a partner and sit back to back with him. They will number themselves off as Partners A and B. Every set of partners will have a bag of LEGO pieces identical to one another. Partner A will have to make something using every piece of LEGO in his bag, and then while neither partner can look at each other's design, Partner A must dictate his design to his partner so that Partner B can try to recreate the design without any visual aid. Once both partners are finished and have looked at each others' results to see what they did correctly/incorrectly, they will repeat the process but with switched roles.

0:05 – 0:30: LEGO Land

Teams play the game.

0:30 – 0:40: Charades

The CITs will be instructed to switch partners. Again, they will choose between them who will be Partner A and who will be Partner B. All Partners A will report to the facilitator and will be given a charade (movie, book, song, etc.). Each person will get the same charade. At the same time, all Partners A will act out their charade for their respective Partners B. The first team to guess correctly wins. Repeat this process switching off between Partners A and B four times.

0:40 – 1:05: Coloring Book

Each CIT will receive a picture from a coloring book (these can be all the same, or each one different). Along with the picture, they will receive a piece of blank paper and a pencil. The CITs will be instructed to decide how they want their picture to be colored, and should write these instructions on the piece of paper. The facilitator will collect all the pictures and sets of instructions, and redistribute them to the group. It is important to ensure that no one has his own picture/instructions. It is also vital that the instructions are handed out with their corresponding pictures. Once all the pictures have been redistributed, the CITs will spend time following the written instructions and will color in the pictures.

1:05 – 1:15: Wrap-Up

The facilitator will lead a short discussion, illustrating the importance of communication among staff and campers. The CITs should be given an opportunity to discuss their feelings about the program—what they found encouraging and what they found frustrating. It is important to reiterate why communication is vital in a camp setting and briefly go through ways to improve communication skills.

Program #6: Communication Barriers

Goals:
- To increase knowledge of roadblocks to communication
- To identify significant aspects of communication

Materials:
- Paper with roadblock roles printed on them

Timed Procedure:

0:00 – 0:05   Assign characters
0:05 – 0:20   Party game
0:20 – 0:35   Debrief party game and discussion about communication roadblocks

DETAILED PROCEDURE

0:00 – 0:05: Assign Characters

Secretly assign characters to each member of the group from the Roadblock Roles list found at the end of this program.

0:05 – 0:20: Party Game

Participants will each take turns role-playing the various roadblock roles. One participant will be deemed the party host in each scene and will have the task of trying to figure out the role that the others are playing and then respond to them to show they understand who they are dealing with. Participants will act out the scene for two to three minutes.

0:20 – 0:35: Debrief Party Game and Discussion About Communication Roadblocks

- Participants will guess who was each character.
- Identify the significant aspects of how each character communicated: tone, body language, direct and indirect messages, word choice, and eye contact.
- What were the impacts and consequences of the traits identified?
- Why it important to be aware of these traits when working with campers?

Roadblock Roles

- Ms. Condescending: Puts campers and staff members down.
- Sergeant: Always directing or ordering other people around.
- Mr. Warning: Constantly threatens to take things away. "If you don't clean up, you won't get a cabin activity.

- Mr. Inappropriate: Always makes the perverted or inappropriate comment.
- Mr. Praising: Counselor does not discipline or say anything negative. He wants to be his camper's best friend.
- Mr. Talker: Overtalkative/Interrupter. He doesn't listen to campers needs.
- Mr. Silence: Person who doesn't respond, He just nods his head.

Program #7: Non-Verbal Communication

Goals:
- To identify the importance of non-verbal behavior
- To introduce the concept of eye contact, posture, proximity, and facial expression.

Materials:
None

Timed Procedure:

0:00 – 0:10   Introduction
0:10 – 0:15   Discussion
0:15 – 0:25   Skill identification
0:25 – 0:35   Non-verbal role-play
0:35 – 0:45   Debrief

DETAILED PROCEDURE

0:00 – 0:10: Introduction

Have two participants conduct a role-play in the front the room, wearing masks (or holding up a sheet of paper in front of their faces). This role-play can be about any topic that the participants offer.

Variation: Triad Role-Play

Have participants get in groups of three and role-play a conversation between a camper and a counselor that may occur at camp. Have the third person give the "counselor" feedback based on the aforementioned skills. Do not provide any feedback based on the content of the discussion.

0:10 – 0:15: Discussion

- What was this experience like for the participants?
- What made this experience challenging?
- What cues do you miss out on when you cannot see the other person?
- Why is non-verbal behavior important?

Some reasoning for the importance of understanding non-verbal behavior: Often people do not state how they are actually feeling. Non-verbal behavior can provide clues to what is going on inside. Non-verbal behavior can convey conflicting or complex feelings. Non-verbal behavior can help convey interest and help us connect to our campers.

0:15 – 0:25: Skill Identification

Have participants identify different types of non-verbal behavior.

- Eye contact: Eye contact conveys attention. However, don't stare into the other person's eyes. Some suggest intervals of four to five seconds of eye contact.
- Body language and posture: Lean slightly forward to show interest. Do not cross arms over chest.
- Mirroring: Match your body posture to that of the other person to whom you are talking, as if they were looking at themselves in the mirror. This technique conveys empathy.
- Proximity: Give someone enough space to feel comfortable. Angle your body toward the person to whom you are speaking. Do not sit directly facing each other.

0:25 – 0:35: Non-Verbal Role-Play

Tell CITs to go off somewhere for five minutes. Each person should spend two minutes talking about themselves. The other person should be instructed that he is not able to respond to anything that the partner says; however, he should do the best to show that he is listening.

0:35 – 0:45: Debrief

When debriefing, ask how participants could tell their partner was listening, even though the partner was not able to respond.

- What was this experience like?
- What was it like to not respond to the your partner?
- How could you tell that your partner was listening?

Program #8: Something to Talk About

Goals:
- To help CITs recognize the importance of looking beyond the words in a conversation
- To help CITs understand the difference between listening and active listening
- To help improve the CIT's active listening skills

Materials:
- Three-minute communications test (Figure 3-1)
- Markers
- Chart paper

Timed Procedure:
0:00 – 0:10   Introduction and communications test
0:10 – 0:25   Body language breakdown
0:25 – 0:40   Active listening tips and activity
0:40 – 0:55   Practicing active listening without problem solving
0:55 – 1:00   Wrap-up

DETAILED PROCEDURE

0:00 – 0:10: Introduction and Communications Test

The facilitator will hand out the three-minute communications test (Figure 3-1) to each CIT. They will be given a few minutes to complete the test. When everyone has finished, the facilitator will count how many people followed the instructions properly. The facilitator will then explain the purpose of the test. The CITs will brainstorm different communication styles, and the facilitator will give a brief introduction to the importance of communication in active listening.

0:10 – 0:25: Body Language Breakdown

Ask for a couple of volunteers to demonstrate different types of gestures often used in communicating. After each gesture is presented, the CITs will discuss what they think that gesture communicates. The facilitator will go through the following list of gestures and their meanings:
- Crossed arms: Sends a message of being closed off
- Leaning slighting forward: Sends a message of being open to conversation
- Making direct eye contact: May be appropriate and demonstrate concentration, or may be too overwhelming for the camper—the CIT should choose how much eye contact to make depending on the camper's reaction

- Looking at other people in the distance while talking to camper: Shows that you are uninterested or are too anxious to deal with the situation by yourself
- Sitting too close: Makes the camper uncomfortable
- Sitting face to face: This can be intimidating for a camper—it is better to sit at a slight angle

0:25 – 0:40: Active Listening Tips and Activity

The facilitator will go through the six tips for active listening and their importance. The CITs will then be broken up into pairs and instructed to choose person A and person B. Person A will then have three minutes to talk about anything that comes to his mind. Person B is instructed not to say anything at all, however, the use of body language is permitted. After the three minutes are up, person B has one minute to respond to what person A said. Then the CITs will repeat the activity, this time with person B speaking and person A listening. After these conversations take place, the CITs will regroup for a mini-discussion on how it felt to be both person A and person B.

Six Tips for Active Listening

- Make eye contact.
- Just listen to what the other person says without thinking about what you are going to say in response. People usually just wait for their turn to talk and don't really hear others.
- Repeat back what the person has said using your own words.
- See if you can identify how the person is feeling.
- Check with the person to see if you "got it right" in terms of understanding their experience.
- Ask clarifying questions if you are not sure about something the other person has said.

0:40 – 0:55: Practicing Active Listening Without Problem Solving

Ask the CITs how active listening is different from problem solving. (Active listening pays attention to the camper's experience, while problem solving attempts to get the camper to solve a problem.) Counselors often jump to problem solving without really understanding the camper's experience.

The CITs will then be divided into six groups and given a scenario where a camper comes to a CIT with a problem. Each group should have two of its members role-playing the campers with a problem or issue, and a CIT who uses active listening skills to make the camper feel heard. It is important that the CIT does not focus on solving the camper's problem. The remaining group members should give the role-players feedback and talk about what it was like to just listen without solving the camper's problem.

0:55 – 1:00: Wrap-Up

The CITs will have an opportunity to ask any questions about active listening and communication. The facilitator will reemphasize how difficult active listening is, but will also state that a positive intent to listen is even more important that the actual skills.

Three-Minute Communications Test

The following test was a product of the work of many of the world's most renowned archeologists. These individuals have managed to decipher the carvings of an ancient Warlock tablet from a cavern near Stonehenge, England. Translated and slightly updated for all extensive purposes, *you will have three minutes to complete this examination.* Please read all of the questions before proceeding.

1. Write your name at the top right-hand corner of this page.
2. Draw a happy face in the top left-hand corner of this page.
3. Sing a line from a Justin Bieber song.
4. Stand up and do 10 full-stride jumping jacks.
5. Give the person on your right and left a hug and tell them how outstanding they are.
6. With your arms over your head, spin and say, "I'm a ballerina," then stop, jump three times saying "1, 2, 3," and then throw your arms out in a finale and yell "Triple sow cow!"
7. Flex your arms and yell, "look how buff I am!"
8. On the left-hand margin of this page, multiply 25 x 6.
9. Divide your answer by 5, and write the new one below your name in the top right corner of this page.
10. Draw a circle around the word "Justin Bieber" in question 3.
11. Sing a verse from your all-time favorite song.
12. Ignore all directions thus far and complete only number 6.
13. Name all the seven dwarfs.
14. Stand up with a grin from ear to ear and proudly say, "I am nearly finished, and I have followed all directions accordingly."
15. Now that you have finished reading all of the above, complete only number 5.

Figure 3-1. Three-minute communications test

Program #9: How Do You Feel?

Goals:
- To introduce to the concept of empathy
- To identify a list of feelings and learn how this is related to empathic communication
- To practice the skill of reflecting

Materials:
None

Timed Procedure:

0:00 – 0:05   Define empathy
0:05 – 0:25   Emotion word single down
0:25 – 0:35   Primary emotions and secondary feelings
0:35 – 0:40   Building empathic responses
0:40 – 0:60   Role-play

DETAILED PROCEDURE

0:00 – 0:05: Define Empathy

Ask the CITs what empathy is and why it is important. If they do not know, provide this definition and then ask why it is important. Then, ask the CITs how they can build empathy. The answer is that the first way to do this is by accurately identifying feelings.

Empathy: The ability to perceive accurately and sensitively the inner feelings of the camper and to communicate his understanding of these feelings in language that fits with the camper's experience.

0:05 – 0:25: Emotion Word Single Down

In groups, give participants two to three minutes to create a list of feeling words. After this step is completed, have each group share take turns sharing the words on their list. If a group shares the word "happy," and another group has this word, they must cross it off their list until only one group is left. In the front of the room, the facilitator should write each feeling word to create a complete feeling list.

0:25 – 0:35: Primary Emotions and Secondary Feelings

Identify the four primary emotions: sacred, happy, sad, and angry. A secondary feeling is one that covers up for a primary feeling. (You usually see the secondary feeling, not the primary one). Anger is often a secondary emotion that covers up for sadness and fear. This recognition is important because when campers seem angry, it is probably because they are sad or sacred of something.

0:35 – 0:40: Building Empathic Responses

The facilitator shares empathetic responses that can be used to explore camper feelings:
- I wonder if… (you are feeling sad)
- It appears that…
- It seems like…
- Let me see if I get it…
- If I catch what you are saying…
- So maybe you feel…

0:40 – 0:60: Role-Play

The CITs get in partners and role-play a situation. The person playing the counselor must be sure to respond to the camper using an empathic response.

Program #10: Guide to Assessing Camper Problems

Goals:
- To teach counselors how to assess problems
- To provide an opportunity to practice this skill

Materials:
None

Timed Procedure:
0:00 – 0:05   Demonstration role-play
0:05 – 0:15   Guiding questions
0:15 – 0:45   CIT role-play

DETAILED PROCEDURE

0:00 – 0:05: Demonstration Role-Play

The CIT advisor should role-play a homesick camper or tell a story about a camper that is homesick. The advisor should then ask the CITs what questions they have about this camper is order to understand what the problem is and how severe it is.

0:05 – 0:15: Guiding Questions

Brainstorm with CITs what questions they can look at to evaluate the problem.

- What is camper's perception of concern?
- How severe is the problem?
- When does the problem surface? *If the problem surfaces during rest time, before bed, or other unstructured time, it is likely the camper is exhibiting anxiety or is homesick.*
- Does the problem become more severe when the camper gets attention? *Often, campers act out more when the counselors are paying attention so that they can "work toward" going home. If campers exhibit isolating behavior or crying when they are not receiving attention, it is less likely to be due to homesickness.*
- How frequent is it? When did it start?
- Is the person harming himself?
- What are the consequences of the problem?
- How has the person tried to cope with the problem?

0:15 – 0:45: CIT Role-Play

CITs should take turns role-playing possible situations that may come up and have other CITs assess the situation.

Program #11: Introduction to Discussion Leading

Goals:
- To learn where to sit when leading a discussion
- To learn how to navigate silence
- To learn basic skills

Materials:
None

Timed Procedure:
0:00 – 0:05   Seating
0:05 – 0:15   Basic skills
0:15 – 0:25   Navigating silence

DETAILED PROCEDURE

0:00 – 0:05: Seating

Tell two CITs that their job is to get everyone seated in order to lead a discussion. Once everyone is seated, tell the leaders to sit where they would sit if they were facilitating the discussion. Then, have the group process their choices for the seating arrangement. Would the group members have seated the group the same way or differently?

Seating Guidelines

- All members should be in a circle.
- The facilitator should be sitting with participants in the circle, not sitting or standing outside or in the middle of the circle.
- Everyone should be on the same level (i.e., all on the floor or all in chairs).
- Co-facilitators should be seated across from each other in the circle. This arrangement allows the leaders to make eye contact with each other so they can play off each other or pass the facilitation to the other person.

0:05 – 0:15: Basic Skills

Ask CITs what skills the group leaders need in order to lead a successful discussion.

Paraphrasing: Repeat back to the group what the camper said, using different words.

Question Stacking: This skill is used when many people raise their hand to speak. The leader should point out the order in which they will call on the individuals so that they can put their hands down.

Guiding: When campers interpret questions in a way that guides the questions away from the main point, you need to clarify or add other questions to get the result you want. You have to continually focus on the main point and what you want them to learn from the conversation.

0:15 – 0:25: Navigating Silence

Pay attention to participant non-verbal cues: Shaking their head to disagree, nodding, making eye contact. These are great to comment on to bring in a camper who is quiet or to help maintain conversation when no one is answering the question.

Leader non-verbal cues: Pointing, "keep going" hand motion, leaning forward to encourage, lean back to create space, making eye contact, "stop/slow down" hand motion.

Navigating silence: Come up with answers to the questions ahead of time, so if there is silence, you can provide your opinion. Another way to navigate silence is let the silence happen, rephrase the question, comment on other people's comments, go back to something specific someone else said, or/and ask more specific questions.

Flexibility: If someone answers a question and takes it to a different direction, do you follow that new direction or stay on course?

Program #12: Practice Discussion Leading

Goals:
- To apply discussion leading skills and put them into practice
- To practice giving and receiving feedback

Materials:
- Practice discussion leading handout (Figure 3-2)

Timed Procedure:

0:00 – 0:10   Recap what CITs have learned
0:10 – 0:20   Break into co-facilitating pairs and prepare for discussion leading
0:20 – 0:30   Discussion 1
0:30 – 0:40   Discussion 2
0:40 – 0:50   Discussion 3

DETAILED PROCEDURE

0:00 – 0:10: Recap What CITs Have Learned

Start by asking CITs to recap what skills they have learned previously:
- Paraphrasing answers
- Steering conversation direction
- Using non-verbal cues
- Navigating silence

Tell CITs that they will be paired into partners and given bullet points from which they will lead a discussion. They should add one or two additional questions that they see as relevant. Some things they should think about with their partner include:
- Who is leading what part of the discussion?
- What is the goal of the program?

0:10 – 0:20: Break Into Co-Facilitating Pairs and Prepare for Discussion Leading

Pair CITs in partners, and provide each group with the practice discussion leading handout (Figure 3-2). They can feel free to add questions to the handout and should keep in mind what they will do if they do not get a response to their question.

0:20 – 0:50: Group Discussions

Create groups of six CITs and one staff member (or whatever works for your program). Groups should take turns leading discussions. After each discussion, staff member and participants should give the leaders feedback. Then group leaders should switch.

Practice Discussion Leading

Discussion 1

Goal: To understand the importance of building a trust with campers

1. How do you define trust?
2. Why is it important to build a trusting relationship between campers and counselors?
3. What is one thing someone can do to build trust with campers?
4. Share an experience of having a counselor you did not trust and what that experience was like.
5. Talk about a counselor that you trusted and what that experience meant to you.

Discussion 2

Goal: To understand the importance of building trust with in the cabin

1. What events happen in the cabin that can destroy trust?
2. Have you ever been in a cabin when members did not trust each other? What was that experience like?
3. What could the counselor have done to facilitate more trust amongst cabinmates?
4. How do you differentiate between a lack of trust in the cabin and "normal" cabin conflicts?
5. How has your experience been different when you were in a cabin that had high levels of trust versus low levels?

Discussion 3

Goal: To explore how to build trust with in the cabin

1. What can you do that will model acceptance of your campers so you can help build trust? Be specific.
2. What can you do if your co-counselors are treating campers in a way that breaks the trust in the cabin?
3. What activities can you do with your cabin that will increase cabin trust?
4. What qualities do you have that can help build trust with in the CIT group?

Figure 3-2. Practice discussion leading handout

4

Knowing Your Campers

Philosophy and Basic Concepts

Filling Up Your Tool Box

One of the major keys to being a successful counselor is how well you know your campers. A camp counselor is not given much time in the very beginning of the summer to know each camper in their cabin really well, which makes the first 48 hours crucial to the counselor. The counselor has to ensure that the campers are adjusting to each other and the camp community, all while learning as much as he possibly can in those first 48 hours. The more information the counselor can collect, the more comfortable the camper will feel right away at camp. The observations the counselor makes are tools for him to work with the campers.

The counselor can start by paying close attention to the clothing the campers wear. More often than not, fashion can be a gateway into a camper's likes, hobbies, and personality. Is your camper wearing a hat? Is your camper wearing a pop culture reference? Is your camper wearing the logo of a sports team? This information can help start conversations between counselors and campers that, for the camper, can really break the ice. Campers then begin to feel like they can get comfortable with their counselor because they are being addressed with topics with which they are already comfortable. When campers get to a comfort zone at camp, it can help curb moments of sadness or homesickness.

Campers' experiences can be significantly different when they have a counselor who uses their observations to get to know them better. The tools a counselor carries around with him arm him to take on many of the events involving the campers that take place in the course of a summer. The more a counselor knows can also help raise the level how the counselor brings campers together as a community. The better a counselor can read each individual camper, the easier it becomes to read the larger group. This understanding will help add to an atmosphere that is caring and welcoming. That will help create a community that feels more like a second home to each camper.

Basic Concepts: The Six Most Important Hours of the Day

The six most important hours of the day are breakfast, lunch, dinner, rest hour, wake-up, and bedtime because they are the times that are the least structured, and thus the times when homesickness arises as well as fighting or bullying. It is helpful to have the CITs observe cabins during these times and learn how to put more structure into these periods of the day. They can do this by creating morning and evening routines, sitting next to a homesick camper at meals, or playing table games when campers are finished eating.

Age Characteristics

It is important to know how campers at different ages differ in interests, maturity, and the type of counselors that they need. It can be helpful to have a panel of counselors come in who work with different age groups. They can speak about the unique needs of working with older or younger kids. Another way to teach CITs about different age characteristics is to have them think back to when they were a certain age. Ask them to reflect on the following:
- How did you feel your first day of camp?
- What were you scared of before/during camp?
- What things made you angry/mad?
- What kind of things did others do that made you sad/left out/uncomfortable?
- What did you enjoy most at camp at this age?

Lastly, you can have CITs interview different age campers about their favorite TV shows, things about camp, and so forth, and then have CITs compare what they learned when meeting different kids to see if they can find patterns about common interests or fears.

Judgments

At some point in the summer, it may be beneficial to explore judgments that come to mind about campers. Often, counselors see a kid as a bully or a nerd without thinking about what struggles the individual is facing. By learning more about how you judge others, you can challenge your beliefs.

Program #13: Awks and Gawks

Goals:
- To help the CITs understand the age-appropriate challenges facing campers in the units with which they will be working
- To provide the CITs with an opportunity to think through coping mechanisms and effective ways of handling campers going through these phases
- To provide CITs with an understanding of what activities campers of this age group are capable of participating in and able to grasp

Materials:
- Eight small pieces of paper—four with male diagram, four with female diagram
- Three pieces of chart paper
- Markers
- Camper Ages and Characteristics handout (Figure 4-1) or Ages and Stages handout (Figure 4-2)
- Gong, bell, or whistle

Timed Procedure:
0:00 – 0:10   Atom
0:10 – 0:20   Small diagrams
0:20 – 0:40   Group discussions
0:40 – 0:50   Presentations
0:50 – 1:05   How to deal
1:05 – 1:10   Wrap-up

DETAILED PROCEDURE

0:00 – 0:10: Atom

As the CITS come in, facilitator will tell them to spend some time mingling, and that when they hear the gong go off they should then get into groups of how ever many number of times the gong was hit (e.g., if the gong goes off four times, they should get into groups of four). Repeat this activity a few times, and then for the last number make sure you have six single-gendered groups. Each group will receive a piece of large butcher paper, on which they will trace a member of their team. Then, give each group a gender and an age. Each group will also receive a marker.

0:10 – 0:20: Small Diagrams

In their small groups, CITs are encouraged to think about their physical, social, and emotional selves at the age to which they've been assigned. On the diagram, they should label what they remember appropriately. (For example, the boys' group may write "soccer" where the feet are, "embarrassment about puberty" in the armpit area, "love logic puzzles" in the brain area). After about five minutes, give each group the Camper Ages and Characteristics handout (Figure 4-1) or the Ages and Stages handout (Figure 4-2). These handouts can help guide them in the process. (The Camper Ages and Characteristics handout is simpler, and the Ages and States handout is more complex. Choose whichever handout will best meet your needs.)

0:20 – 0:40: Group Discussions

Have each female group switch diagrams with a male group. Each group should go through the diagrams of the other group and determine the main issues presented for the other gender and age. They should compile a list and have it ready to present.

0:40 – 0:50: Presentations

Each group will be given a few minutes to present their findings to the other groups. After their presentation, the audience will critique their key points and offer their perspective.

0:50 – 1:05: How to Deal

After both groups have presented and critiqued, the CITs will have an opportunity to brainstorm and share tips on how to deal with problems that may arise with campers as a result of age-related issues. Going around the room, everyone will have an opportunity to share (if they'd like). They may choose to share an experience they had as a camper or student at this age, and suggest a method that proved effective or what they would have benefited from at this time. The facilitator will go through the Ages and Stages handout (Figure 4-2) and cover any topics not hit on or elaborate where necessary. CITs are encouraged to ask any questions they may have.

1:05 – 1:10 Wrap-Up

Camper Ages and Characteristics

Ages 8 to 10

Physical	Social	Emotional/Intellectual
Muscles are growing.	Very dependent on counselor guidance	Self-conscious about underdeveloped skills
Girls mature faster than boys.	Like pretend games	Strong parental attachment
Some girls mature earlier than others.	Follow rules out of respect	Short attention span
A lot of energy	Want everything to be fair	Fearful in new environment until they are comfortable

Campers need structure and are likely to experience homesickness and bedwetting.

Ages 11 to 13

Physical	Social	Emotional/Intellectual
Exhibit differing degrees of sexual maturity	Concerned with being "cool"	Conscious about bodily changes
Hormones and emotions increase.	Number of cliques increase	Concerned about being part of the group
Girls increase concern about body image	Care about equality in counselor's affection	Want independence and guidance
Wide gender gap in terms of physical development	Arguments between peers increase	Less interested in fantasy and more interested in abstract reasoning

Bullying and feeling left out is more common.
Many kids still experience homesickness.

Figure 4-1. Camper Ages and Characteristics handout

Camper Ages and Characteristics

Ages 14 to 17

Physical	Social	Emotional/Intellectual
Girls tend to watch weight	Males and females socialize more.	Begin to accept individuality
Concerned about body image	Search for intimacy	Develop empathy and perspective taking abilities
Increased physical strength	Leadership roles	Less patience with meaningless activities
	Can complete tasks with less guidance from counselor	Better able to manage new situations

Group acceptance is important. Eating disorders occur more frequently. Campers can partake in long-term projects.

Reference: Blackstock, B. & Latimer, J. (1975). *Camp Counsellor's Handbook.* Canada: Gage Educational Publishing.

Figure 4-1. Camper Ages and Characteristics handout (cont.)

Ages and Stages: Child and Youth Development

What follows is a summary of the general characteristics of children at various ages. Since each child is an individual, you may expect wide variations from the "average" child as indicated here. Children who vary from the general pattern, and you will have some in your cabin, should not be considered abnormal. However, should their physical development be radically different from their bunkmates, you may have to do some special work with that child to make him feel more at ease with the group. This includes both those children who are physically and emotionally very advanced for their age as well as those who lag somewhat behind.

Eight-Year-Olds	**Nine-Year-Olds**	**10-Year-Olds**
Physical Growth		
The tempo of the child is fast: she does everything in high gear; she is expansive and boisterous. The maturity level of boys and girls begins to draw apart. Tends to show strong admiration for teacher and parent. Courage and daring are characteristics, as well as spontaneity.	Works and plays hard. Skillful in motor performances and likes to display skill. Great interest in competitive sports, (e.g., baseball). Apt to "overdo," and has difficulty in calming down. Differences between boys and girls begin to widen.	Girls same average height as boys, but are growing faster. Most girls have heard about menstruation. In boys, little trace of sexual maturation or interest in sex. In both boys and girls, some interest in "smutty" jokes.
Tension Outlets		
Whole energy is directed toward social motor activities. Most common outlet is the need to urinate when taxed with something he doesn't like or feels unequal to.	Fewer gross tensional outlets, mostly small things (e.g., picking at cuticle and running fingers through hair). Boys especially need to "let off steam."	Stomachaches and headaches common. Nail biting, stuttering, fiddling with things. Eating common tensional outlet. Some seem to be in constant physical motion.

Figure 4-2. Ages and Stages handout

Ages and Stages: Child and Youth Development

Eight-Year-Olds	Nine-Year-Olds	10-Year-Olds
Friends and Associations		
Less insistence on having own way, less worry about behavior of others. Unsupervised play may result in dissension. Tries to work out relationships so that everyone is happy. Can take part in competitive games and can sometimes lose with grace. Not ready for complex rules. Begins to have best friend, and prefers to play with same sex.	Tendency to have special friends and to choose a member of same sex for this friend. Open criticism of opposite sex. Enjoys group play that shows organization (e.g., ball). Likes clubs with purpose, including secret hideouts, but they do not last. Many enjoy scout-type activities under adult supervision.	Boys mingle easily with each other. True friendships possible. Girls' relationships are tense and emotional: intrigue, secrecy, conspiracy. Little fighting or arguing. Little interest in opposite sex. Sex lines cross fairly freely.
Ethical Sense		
Great interest in possessions and money. Likes to acquire and barter. May take money or things if she "needs" them. Tendency toward tale-telling and boasting. But truthfulness about matters a child considers important.	Essentially truthful and honest. Honesty not consistent. May think it worse to lie to father than to others. Receptive to elementary ideas of justice. Lays stress on who started problem, and wants blame apportioned fairly.	10-year-olds tend to be more concerned about wrong than right. And he is somewhat more concerned about the wrongs of others than his own. Dependence shown on mother.

Figure 4-2. Ages and Stages handout (cont.)

Ages and Stages: Child and Youth Development

11-Year-Olds	12-Year-Olds	13-Year-Olds
Physical Growth		
Girls beginning to mature rapidly, 90 percent of mature stature achieved. Beginning of sexual maturation. Boys more uniform in growth pattern than girls, but few show sexual maturation. 80 percent of mature height achieved. Fat period begins. Both show more interest in sex.	Girls have period of fastest growth in height and weight. Breasts begin to fill out; menstruation begins at the end of this year, beginning of next. Boys show marked differences. Puberty begins. Girls show much interest in menstruation, but secretive. Boys' sexual interests: books, "dirty" words, etc.	Girls' rapid growth begins to slow. Boys begin real puberty with deepening voice, rapid sexual development. Most rapid growth. Most girls have menstruated and accept it as natural. Boys are modest about being seen in the nude.
Tension Outlets		
Similar to 10-year-olds, with stomachaches, nail biting, facial twitches, much bodily motion, arm waving. Constant motion.	Symptoms similar to 11-year-olds. Much oral overflow: giggling, vulgar laughter, loud noises, anger outbursts, stamping around, spurts of intense activity.	Calming of tensional outlets. More small tics and twitches. Moodiness and withdrawal takes place of gross physical activity. Periods of intense effort related to one special activity.

Figure 4-2. Ages and Stages handout (cont.)

Ages and Stages: Child and Youth Development

11-Year-Olds	12-Year-Olds	13-Year-Olds
Friends and Associations		
Boys more selective in choosing playmates. Quarreling and making up, but not as intense as with girls. Girls watch each other closely and try to control each other; verbal battles and "not speaking." Some interest in boys by girls, although "anti-boy" feelings common. Boys neutral about girls. Teasing common.	Both boys and girls tend to have large groups of friends. Boys and girls mingle in rather formless groups.	Boys less sociable than at 12, less group spirit, more interest in solitary activity. One or two close friends. Girls are critical and argumentative with friends. Boys become "women haters," and girls find boys their own age immature; they gravitate toward older boys.
Ethical Sense		
Begins to steer own course, and wants freedom to be a non-conformist. Not as rigid as she was at 10. Influenced by her feelings in ethical situations. In truthfulness, thinks first of her own protection.	More level-headed than 11-year-olds in approach to ethical problems. Can weigh pros and cons. Sensitive to opinion of peers; has developed sense of fairness and truth. Shows less dependence on adults.	Thinks about ethical conduct of others. Less apt to think of himself alone. Takes more factors into account. Takes intellectual interest in ethical questions.
Reference: URJ Camp George Staff Manual, 2005		

Figure 4-2. Ages and Stages handout (cont.)

Program #14: Guess Who?

Goals:
- To provide the CITs with an understanding of watching what you say around others
- To help the CITs recognize the diverse community that exists inside the camp environment
- To raise awareness among the CITs of the importance of not making judgments based on physical characteristics
- To help the CITs become more mindful in their everyday language

Materials:
- Two pieces of poster board (to create one Guess Who game set)
- Three sets of 30 pictures of children
- 30 index cards
- Post-it® notes
- Tape
- Guess Who questions (Figure 4-3)

Game Board Preparation:
Retrieve pictures from modeling websites on the Internet or free stock photos. Paste one set of pictures on each piece of poster board. Paste the remaining pictures onto index cards. Participants will use the Post-its to cover up the pictures when they think that a particular camper does not meet criteria to be the match (this step is done in lieu of putting down the game piece on the traditional game board).

Timed Procedure:
0:00 – 0:10   Settle in and divide into groups
0:10 – 0:15   Explanation of the game
0:15 – 0:50   Guess Who?
0:50 – 1:05   Discussion
1:05 – 1:10   Wrap-up

DETAILED PROCEDURE

0:00 – 0:10: Settle in and Divide Into Groups

The CITs will divide themselves into groups of three to four people. Groups should include mixed gender; at least one girl and one boy should be in each group.

0:10 – 0:15: Explanation of the Game

The CITs will be given a basic explanation of how to play the game Guess Who? Each group will receive a game board with 30 pictures of kids displayed on the board. There will be a deck of cards, each card displaying one of the kids from the game board. There will be 30 cards in total. Each group selects a card, and using a post it should cover the matching picture on their board. Unlike in the real game of Guess Who?, the teams are not asking questions based on physical appearances; they will be asking the Guess Who questions provided in Figure 4-3 that assess personality, background, and experiences. They will have to give answers based on what they can see in the pictures of each camper. The questions will be provided, but only "Yes" or "No" answers can be given. Each team will ask questions until they have, by process of elimination, only one child left on their board.

0:15 – 0:50: Guess Who?

Play the game. When all but one picture has been covered, a team has arrived at an answer. The facilitator will check to see if they have guessed correctly. Facilitator will keep score of which teams guess correctly/incorrectly. The CITS will play until all teams have had a chance to play.

0:50 – 1:05: Discussion

Facilitate a discussion about judging campers based on their experiences, personalities, looks, and backgrounds.

Discussion Points

- In cabin meetings, you learn a great deal of information about your campers' mental health, physical health, and home life. Take this into account when interacting with them, but refrain from using this information as a judging tool.
- Kids in camp are coming from a wide variety of backgrounds and experiences, and it is important to use that as a positive thing; celebrate differences, and work to create an entirely new community for all of your kids together.
- It is important to be cautious of the language used around camp and in front of campers.
- The photos used in this program are of real kids whom the group has never met before. The photos were found online. This just proves that it is very easy to judge real people based on what they look like.

Discussion Questions

- How did you guys feel when you saw the list of questions?
- What made this activity challenging?
- Why do you think you chose to cover certain pictures when questions were asked? What drove you to choose those kids in response to the questions you were asked?
- Was this activity ever easy?

- What are some things you have learned from this activity?
- How does this lesson apply to your cabin? To your age group? To our general camp community?

1:05 – 1:10: Wrap-Up

The facilitator will read the Guess Who's Coming to Camp? list to reinforce the diversity of the different types of kids who will be living in the camp environment this summer.

Guess Who's Coming to Camp?

Only-child campers
Campers from one-parent homes
Campers with eating disorders
Campers with physical disabilities
Campers with learning disabilities
Campers who have failed a grade
Campers who developed early
Campers who developed late
Campers with gay or lesbian parents
Adopted campers
Campers with sick family members
Campers who have gone through traumatic experiences
Campers who are new to camp
Confident campers
Anxious campers
Quiet campers
Smelly campers
Campers who wet the bed
Campers who run away
Campers who have been in the hospital
Sexually active campers
Healthy campers
Energetic campers
Campers with too much energy
Musical campers
Athletic campers
Shy campers

Campers from interfaith families
Know-it-all campers
Rude campers
Poor campers
Rich campers
Campers who think they are beautiful
Campers who think they are ugly
Campers who have been bullied
Campers who are bullies
Campers who come to camp because their parents force them to
Campers who are afraid to go home
Campers with divorced parents
Homosexual campers
Interracial campers
Campers who are at camp on a scholarship or financial assistance

What kind of camper were you?

Guess Who? Questions

Is your camper the type of kid who:

1. Comes from a blended family?
2. Is popular at school?
3. Is questioning his sexuality?
4. Wishes he were taller?
5. Wishes he were shorter?
6. Counts calories?
7. Has a single parent?
8. Gets homesick easily?
9. Wets the bed?
10. Is overly sensitive?
11. Has ADHD?
12. Punches people to express anger?
13. Craves attention?
14. Can't afford new clothes?
15. Thinks no one will like him?
16. Has trouble seeing the brighter side of things?
17. Does really well in school?
18. Struggles to pass his classes?
19. Wishes he had siblings?
20. Will develop before everyone else in his class?
21. Will develop later than everyone else in his class?
22. Thinks he is fat?
23. Has medical issues?
24. Is allergic to peanuts?
25. Thinks he is better than everyone else?
26. Never cries?
27. Everybody loves?
28. Nobody loves?
29. Is sexually active?
30. Is afraid of members of the opposite sex?
31. Has been abused?
32. Needs to be using deodorant?
33. Likes to read?
34. Can't read?
35. Is too mature for his age?
36. Hates to be touched?
37. Gets everything he wants?
38. Has never been told "No"?
39. Is considered "normal"?
40. Drinks alcohol?
41. Uses drugs?
42. Smokes cigarettes?
43. Has traveled?
44. Sleeps with a teddy bear?
45. Is a whiz with technology?
46. Eats a lot?
47. Has a non-Jewish parent?
48. Steals?
49. Tests limits?
50. You might be scared of?
51. Lives in an apartment building?
52. Rejects authority?
53. Has a nanny?
54. Doesn't have grandparents?
55. Has young parents?
56. Has old parents?
57. Parents are still married?
58. Parents are married, but not to each other?
59. Siblings have their own children?
60. Is unpopular?
61. Suffers from anxiety?
62. Is afraid of heights?
63. Doesn't want to be at camp?
64. Counts down the days until camp?
65. Takes regular medication?
66. Suffers from depression?
67. Hates school?
68. Is an insomniac?
69. Is lonely?
70. Is a video-gamer?
71. Is homophobic?
72. Has overprotective parents?
73. Is sheltered?
74. Lives in the suburbs?
75. Lives in the inner city?
76. Is at camp on a scholarship?
77. Has moved around a lot?
78. Comes from a two-income family?
79. Has siblings who are much older or much younger?
80. Has a hearing impairment?

Figure 4-3. Guess Who? questions

Program #15: The Other Side of the Tracks

Goals:
- To raise awareness of stereotypes and assumptions among the CITs
- To encourage the CITs usage of proper terminology
- To increase CITs understanding of being placed in stereotypical categories
- To encourage CITs to think proactively

Materials:
- Pencils
- Other Side worksheets (created by the facilitator)

Timed Procedure:
0:00 – 0:05   Introduction
0:05 – 0:15   Writing instruction and exercise
0:15 – 0:40   The Other Side of the Tracks exercise
0:40 – 1:05   Discussion
1:05 – 1:10   Wrap-up

DETAILED PROCEDURE

0:00 – 0:05: Introduction

The CITs will walk into the room and on their way in will receive a pencil and a piece of paper with four words on it. The facilitator will create five different versions of the Other Side worksheet, each version containing a different set of four words. For example, for Version 1, the facilitator will print a sheet of paper with the words *Divorced, White, Thin,* and *Vegetarian* on it, leaving room under each word for the participant to write his associations. Following is a list of the words for the five versions of the Other Side worksheet:

Version 1	Version 2	Version 3	Version 4	Version 5
Divorced	Single Parent	Rich	Poor	Girl
White	Black	Boy	Fat	Alcohol User
Thin	Heterosexual	Jew	Christian	Homosexual
Vegetarian	Atheist	Tall	Drug User	Short

The facilitator will pass out all five versions of the worksheet, each CIT receiving only one version of the worksheet (i.e. they will only be writing responses for four words). As the worksheets are handed out, the CITs receive no other instruction other than to sit down and remain quite. Once everyone is settled the program will continue.

0:05 – 0:15: Writing Instruction and Exercise

The CITs will receive the instructions to the exercise. They will be told to look at the four words on their paper and to write down the first three words they think of when they read the word. They will do this for each word on the paper, leaving them with 12 newly written words. For example, a piece of paper will contain the words: Divorced, White, Thin, and Vegetarian. The CITs will write three words that they think of when they read the word Divorced and will repeat the process with the words White, Thin, and Vegetarian. When they have completed the activity, they will return their sheet of paper to the facilitator and quietly sit back down.

0:15 – 0:40: The Other Side of the Tracks Exercise

When all of the papers have been collected, the CITs will be instructed to form a horizontal line facing the facilitator. Silence is expected throughout this entire process. After a line has been formed, the CITs will be introduced to the concept of "the track," which is an invisible horizontal line existing right in front of the line they have just formed. The facilitator will read the first of the 20 words out loud and the CITs will be instructed to cross the track if they or anyone they know can identify with the word read in any way. Once they are standing on the other side of the track, the CITs are instructed to face those still standing in the original line and maintain eye contact. Once all those who feel the need to cross the track have crossed, the facilitator will then read out all the words written by the CITs corresponding with that word. After all the written words have been read, the CITs will be told to go back to the original line and the facilitator will continue with the next word. This process will be repeated with each of the 20 words.

0:40 – 1:05: Discussion

After the activity is finished, the CITs will engage in a discussion about their feelings toward the exercise and some of the words brought up in the activity. They will discuss why these stereotypes exist and what can be done to combat them.

1:05 – 1:10: Wrap-Up

The facilitator will reiterate the importance of inclusive language and thoughts and remind all CITs to be conscious of what they say and do around the campers.

5

Managing Camper Behavior

Philosophy and Basic Concepts

This chapter provides the basic information on how to deal with issues that come up during camp. Please consult with your camp director or manual to learn the specific policies at your camp. The information in this section is provided for the CIT director's knowledge. Appropriate information from this section can be used as a foundation to create programs and is often successful when used with role-play.

Basic Concepts

Assessing the Problem

These problems should *never* be handled individually by a CIT. These issues should be shared with the appropriate person in the hierarchy as quickly as possible:
- Suicidal talk, hinting, or action
- Active cutting
- Any type of physical aggression
- Anytime the health and safety of a camper is in question
- Talk or signs of any kind of abuse that occur in the home

Problems that require collaboration with the appropriate staff person and should be shared within 24 hours:
- Eating disorders in which health is not in immediate jeopardy
- Depression that has no hints of suicide
- Prolonged homesickness
- Serious stress or anxiety, related to any issue

Possible signs of camper distress include:
- Inappropriate touching
- Withdrawal
- Excessive worrying
- Not eating
- Body bruises
- Fear of discipline
- Defensiveness
- Excessive sleeping
- Insufficient sleep
- Crying
- Anger
- Somatic complaints
- Shyness
- Need to be center of attention
- Physical aggression

Bullying

Three different people are often involved in bullying: the bully, the victim, and the bystander. The three different types of bullying are: direct bullying (open attacks on a victim), indirect bullying (social isolation and exclusion from a group), and passive bullying (those who participate in bullying but do not usually take the initiative).

It is necessary to not let bullying go unnoticed. When intervening with bullies, immediately describe the behavior that you saw, explain the consequences for their actions, and enforce the consequences. Look for opportunities to help bullies develop positive ways of interacting with the victim.

When intervening with the victim, tell child that you have noticed the bullying behavior and that you want to help. Let the child know that if he is being picked on, it isn't his fault. Encourage the child to express how he has felt when others have excluded him. Ask the child to let you know when it happens again.

Conflict Mediation

Conflict mediation is an important skill for counselors to learn in order to help manage issues that arise at camp. One of the most important things to teach is the difference between mediation and arbitration. Most counselors think that mediation means being the judge. Mediation is really helping campers come to a consensus and increasing their ability to problem solve.

Cutting

Campers engage in cutting for many different reasons. Some campers cut in order to release overwhelming emotions such as anxiety, depression, loneliness, or feelings or being out of control. Others cut to connect with their emotions. They may feel numb, and they use cutting as a way of feeling. Some people cut to self-soothe or self-punish. Most people who cut do not want to kill themselves. It is very important that this information is passed on to the appropriate person in a timely manner. The CIT needs to stay calm and be empathic to the camper. It is especially important to thank the camper for sharing this information, as it must have been tough for the camper.

For the camp director: A camper who cuts should first be sent to the nurse or doctor to check their wounds. Depending on camp rules, a camper can be sent home, or the director can let them stay at camp on the premise that they will refrain from cutting for the remainder of the camp session. A call should be made to inform the parents of the camper's cutting. If the camp cannot keep the camper safe, he must be sent home.

Death

When a camper experiences a death, ask about the camper's loved one. People usually want to talk about it. Ask the camper about the feelings he is experiencing or memories with that person.

Depression

Depression at camp is a tricky one. It is important to assess if the camper is depressed at home as well as at camp. If the camper is not depressed at home, depression may result from homesickness or social anxiety. A general rule of thumb is that if a person is depressed at home and at camp, and he is not suicidal, then there is not much for the counselor to do. The camper would be depressed wherever he is. At least at camp, he is socializing with others, and may have a greater chance to engage in pleasurable activities than at home.

Divorce

Children who have parents who are divorcing or who are divorced often feel as if they are different from all of their peers. Camp is often a place for them because they can feel like they are similar to their peers. CITs must be careful with the language that they use and not assume that everyone lives with both their mom and dad. If a camper is struggling with this issue, take the time to ask them if they want to talk.

Eating Disorders

Eating disorders is a common issue that surfaces at camp. If a camper comes to discuss this issue to a CIT, the most important thing to do is take the time to listen to the camper's concerns. The CIT should tell camper that he must inform the counselor about what he has shared. The most important thing to do when an eating disorder surfaces is to inform the appropriate person in the camp hierarchy, and make sure that a call is made to the parents so that they are informed about the camper's habits. At that time, the appropriate camp person should determine if the camper is appropriate for camp.

Homesickness

A major part of homesickness is insecurity in the environment and feelings of uncertainty in what the day will be like, who the camper will sit next to, and what the camper will do during unstructured time. Campers are usually the most homesick during wake-up, bedtime, mealtimes, and rest hour. Create structure for your cabin by programming during downtimes, posting a schedule, pairing campers up for the day, and keeping the same routine.

Homesickness if often translated into somatic complaints. The child can pretend to be sick, or can experience so much anxiety that they truly experience the physical symptoms. This is most often seen through vomiting, but can also be seen through fever, colds, or body pains. If these symptoms surface, consult with the camp doctor and share that the child has been homesick to help determine the cause and function of the symptom.

Listen to the concerns of the homesick camper, validate those concerns, and try to get him excited about all the things that camp has to offer. Try to keep the conversation short. The more time you give the camper, the more he will become emotional and think about home. Never mention going home or calling mom as an option. The most effective intervention is telling the camper, "You are not going home." If you tell the camper that you will check in with him in an hour, he will try to "prove" how homesick he is so that the counselor/director will send him home.

For the camp director: If a camper's behavior does not improve within one to two days after being told that he cannot go home, this is a good time to assess if camp is a good match for him. If a camper is enjoying himself during some times of the day, you can usually try to keep him at camp. If the camper does not enjoy anything at all, you should probably send him home. In terms of calling parents, it is wise to call the parents and letting them know that their child is homesick by the third day of camp. At this time, the parents are receiving letters asking to be picked up from camp. It shows responsibility on the camp's part to inform the parents prior to them receiving letters and to let them know that it takes many campers one to three days to adjust to camp.

Questioning Sexuality

When a camper discusses his sexual orientation, staff should provide unconditional acceptance. If a camper comes out to a CIT, he should not push to camper to come out to other people or intervene in cabin dynamics. The CIT should listen to the camper, validate his feelings, and see if he wants to be connected to someone else to talk to.

Suicidal Thoughts

Suicidal thoughts or suggestions should be immediately referred to a camp director, unit head, or appropriate camp personnel. If a camper discloses that he is having suicidal thoughts, do not leave the camper alone at any time until the director or appropriate camp personnel has been notified and the individual is assessed.

For the camp director: The main things to assess when working with a camper who has suicidal thoughts are: Does the camper have a specific plan to kill themselves? On a scale of 1 to 10, how likely does the camper rate his ability to follow through with the plan? How feasible or possible is the plan in being successful? (Is the person's plan to jump off a bridge or jump off their bunk?)

If the camper is likely to follow through with the plan, the camper should be sent home. If not, the parents should be informed, and the director and parents should discuss whether the child is appropriate for camp.

Program #16: Setting Consequences

Goals:
- To learn how to intervene with difficult campers
- To understand the most beneficial way to hold camper's accountable for their behavior

Materials:
- Consequences and rewards handout (Figure 5-1)

Timeline:
0:00 – 0:10   Discussion of criticism
0:10 – 0:30   Discuss possible scenarios and interventions in small groups
0:30 – 0:45   Share scenarios and interventions as a large group
0:45 – 0:60   Introduce the consequences and rewards handout

DETAILED PROCEDURE

0:00 – 0:10: Discussion of Criticism

Discuss and evaluate the following views of criticism. Which is the most important? Why?

- Criticism of others needs to be carefully considered rather than spontaneous.
- Criticism must be given privately and not publicly. Shame must not be part of the process.
- You must not give up, but try over and over again.
- Anger has no place in this process. Rebuke must be done out of love.
- If a person sees another doing something bad, that person should tell him and attempt to return him to the right way.

0:10 – 0:30: Discuss Possible Scenarios and Interventions in Small Groups

CITS are divided into groups. Each group comes up with a situation in camp where a camper/a group of campers needs to be rebuked. This situation can be something that happened to them, or something that they would not know how to handle. Have the group move through the interventions listed and discuss which ones might work and why.

0:30 – 0:45: Share Scenarios and Interventions as a Large Group

0:45 – 0:60: Introduce the Consequences and Rewards Handout

Consequences

Please come up with a situation in camp where a camper/group of campers needs to be reprimanded.

Intervention Scenarios:

1. The evil eye (just looking at him)
2. Moving in on the camper (moving closer to him)
3. Proximity (sitting right next to him)
4. Eye contact and "No" headshake (look at him with a look of disappointment)
5. Let's talk about this later (putting him on notice)
6. "Can you do that? Thanks." (a simple request)
7. Changing location (move him away from whoever is involved)
8. "Is this the right place for that?" (pointing out inappropriateness)
9. I-statements (Feeling statement: "When you do that it makes me feel…")
10. Enforceable statements ("You will not do…")
11. Providing choices ("If you do this, then…")
12. Removing camper to time-out (move him away from everyone)
13. Evaluating time-out (after time-out, evaluate what has happened)
14. Utilizing group punishment (all campers participate or lose out on something)
15. Use of the unit head (inform the unit head, and let him know you did this)
16. Meeting with the unit head (actual face to face)
17. Creating a new plan (nothing else so far has worked)
18. Applying consequences (related to the behavior)
19. Contact parents (serious measure)
20. Leave camp (last resort)

Figure 5-1. Consequences and rewards handout

How to Use Rewards and Consequences

Rewards

Individual Camper Rewards: If you have a difficult camper, the best way to improve his behavior is to *catch him doing something good and praise him.*

Collective Cabin Rewards: It is *always* okay to give collective rewards.

List of Possible Rewards

- Extra flashlight time after lights out
- Having lunch with another cabin
- Outdoor cabin activity
- Extra 5 to 10 minutes of cabin activity
- Extra 5 minutes to sleep in
- Choice of a staff member to sit with at a meal
- Two choices of cabin activity and let them pick
- Having a movie on computer during rest hour
- An announcement at lunch, praising the cabin

Consequences

Campers will not resent you for giving consequences. The following chart provides some outlines some simple consequences and follow-up for common camper behaviors. Please note the following steps leading up to using a consequence:
- Step 1: Ask the camper to do something (or not to do something).
- Step 2: Repeat your directive, and state a reward or consequence.
- Step 3: Implement the consequence.

Note on collective consequences: Do *not* use collective consequences unless everyone that is subject to the consequence was "guilty" of the crime.

Figure 5-1. Consequences and rewards handout (cont.)

Examples of Consequences

Time of Day	Behavior	Consequence	Follow-Up
Wake-Up	Repeatedly late getting out of the cabin for breakfast	Camper sets up the table the next morning for breakfast	Alert unit leaders.
		Camper loses 10 minutes off bedtime that night (because they clearly need more sleep)	
Meals	Consistently eating like a slob	Camper eats outside for 5 to 10 minutes	
	Camper is consistently greedy, taking food without sharing	Camper gets food last	
	Camper consistently avoids/refuses to help with table clean up	Camper must do table clean-up for one meal by himself	
Downtime in Cabin	Camper makes fun of, name calls, or pushes another camper	Camper has 5- to 10-minute "time-out" away from other campers (if cabin mates are inside, send camper outside)	• Check in with "victim." • Alert unit leaders.
	Camper consistently excludes peer from joining card game	Camper is not allowed to play card game for the rest of the day	Check in with the instigator to make sure he understands the impact of exclusion.
Activity	Camper repeatedly complains that the activity is stupid	Camper loses 10 minutes of favorite activity (because everyone participates in everything at camp, and if the camper doesn't want to participate in something that isn't his favorite, then he can't participate in his favorite activity, either)	

Figure 5-1. Consequences and rewards handout (cont.)

	Examples of Consequences		
Time of Day	**Behavior**	**Consequence**	**Follow-Up**
Activity	Camper is disruptive by talking with friends	• First time: Separate camper from friends • Second time: Camper spends 5 to 10 minutes of free choice where his counselor is stationed	
	Camper engages in attention-seeking behavior	Camper has a 5- to 10-minute time-out away from other campers, counselors should *not* give him any attention and *will* be mindful of giving praise for appropriate behavior	
Bedtime	Camper consistently makes noise in the cabin to keep others awake	Camper has 10-minute time-out outside the cabin (where a staff member can see him but doesn't talk to him)	• Establish a procedure for how other campers can let staff know about this. • Alert unit leaders if it becomes a pattern of behavior.
	Camper talks about inappropriate things (such as sexual topics)		Alert unit leaders.
Chart co-created with Andrew Benkendorf, LCSW			

Figure 5-1. Consequences and rewards handout (cont.)

Program #17: Bully for You

Adapted from a program written by Lauren Viner.

Goals:
- To familiarize the CITs with the camp's approach to bullying
- To provide CITs with the tools to recognize signs of the bully and the victim, as well as learn strategies for handling bullying situations
- To help the CITs recognize the whole-camp approach to bullying

Materials:
- Song "Don't Laugh at Me" (by Peter, Paul, and Mary)
- Copies of "The Torn Heart" story (Figure 5-2) for staff members
- A large cut-out of a heart
- Signs for the doors
- Post-its (two different colors)
- Golf pencils
- Chart paper
- Markers
- The Facts of Bullying (Figure 5-3)
- Bullying scenarios (Figure 5-4)
- Six to eight staff members (to help facilitate)

Timed Procedure:

0:00 – 0:10	Introduction
0:10 – 0:30	"Don't Laugh at Me"
0:30 – 0:45	Input
0:45 – 1:15	Identification
1:15 – 1:30	Strategize
1:30 – 1:40	Wrap-up and debrief

DETAILED PROCEDURE

0:00 – 0:10: Introduction

The CITs will enter a room where signs will be on the doors, which say things such as:
- Ridicule-free zone
- No dissing here
- Don't laugh at me
- Respect each other

Before the program even begins, the facilitator will explain the sensitive nature of the program and will remind the CITs of the "safe space" rule. If at any time someone feels as though they cannot handle the material being covered, they are free to excuse themselves. The CITs will then be asked to think about put-downs and impact they (the put-downs) can have on a child. The facilitator will ask the CITs to sit down and have the staff members act out "The Torn Heart" story (Figure 5-2), which will include a narrator who tears the heart. After the story, the facilitator will ask the CITs to share the possible consequences of put-downs.

0:10 – 0:30: "Don't Laugh at Me"

The facilitator will explain to the CITs that this song was performed by Peter, Paul, and Mary, and will ask them to listen carefully to the lyrics and whether or not there is any part of the song with which they can identify—either as a bully or as someone who has been bullied. The facilitator will play the song, after which she will ask the CITs to turn to the people near them and discuss for three minutes the following questions:
- What feelings did the song bring up for you?
- What lyrics stood out to you?
- What images came to mind?
- Think about camp (this or another one) or school. Are kids ever unkind to one another? How?
- What have you seen others do to ensure everyone's physical or emotional safety?
- What would the perfect camp look like if there were no bullying?

The CITs will be given some time to think of a time when they were bullied or have bullied someone else. They will be asked to write down on a yellow Post-it what happened and any emotions they may have experienced at the time. The facilitator will stress anonymity. The CITs will then be asked to think of a time when someone made them feel good about themselves and will be instructed to write of this situation on a blue (or different color) Post-it. Again, the facilitator will stress anonymity.

The facilitator will explain to the CITs that a major goal at camp is to ensure that none of the campers have reasons to write yellow Post-its. The facilitator will stress the importance of creating opportunities for situations like those on the blue Post-its to happen.

0:30 – 0:45: Input

The Facts of Bullying (Figure 5-3) will be addressed during this discussion. On a piece of chart paper, the CITs will staff brainstorm the following questions:
- What is bullying?
- Who is involved?
- What does the bully look like?
- What does bullying sound like?

0:45 – 1:15: Identification

The CITs will be divided into groups of six and will be assigned a group facilitator (staff member). The staff members will be assigned different scenarios and rotate between the groups to break down the bullying scenarios (Figure 5-4). The staff members will be given a card with a statement or common bullying situation on it. Staff will be asked to read the card and then discuss with the CITs what they think the situation was trying to focus on:

- The different people involved (bully, victim, and bystander)
- Types of bullying
- What staff can do to help
- How to be proactive against the type of bullying

1:15 – 1:30: Strategize

The CITs will then regroup and spend some time brainstorming ideas of how to handle bullying situations.

Possible Strategies

- Establish consequences for bullying (talk with staff/unit head or call home).
- Be consistent with how you record, report, and prevent bullying.
- Pair unpopular children with helpful and friendly children.
- Encourage and affirm children when they demonstrate helpful behavior.
- Play cooperative games with children.

Intervening With Victims

- Tell the child that you have noticed certain behavior and want to help.
- Let the child know that if he is being picked on, it isn't his fault.
- Encourage the child to express how he has felt when others have excluded him.
- Ask the child to let you know when it happens again.

Intervening With Bullies

- Describe the behavior that you saw.
- Explain and enforce consequences.
- Look for opportunities to help bullies develop positive ways of interacting with the victim.

1:30 – 1:40: Wrap-Up and Debrief

The facilitator will explain to the CITs that the best approach is a whole-camp approach. As a camp, the understanding is that campers bully each other and that it can be prevented. Unfortunately, bullying can be staff-staff and even staff-camper. As role models to these children, staff and CITs must have an understanding that they will respect one another and their campers and treat others how they would want to be treated. The facilitator will also emphasize the point that the CITs are not responsible for solving bullying situations they may come across in their placements, but that they should be aware of how to recognize situations and ensure that they inform the staff of any situations they may come across.

The Torn Heart

One Tuesday morning, when the alarm clock rang, Pedro did not get out of his bunk. Ten minutes later, his counselor opened the door to his cabin.

"Come on," he said. "You'll be late for breakfast again."

"But Jimmy, I'm tired," Pedro said.

"Don't be such a baby," Jimmy said impatiently. (RIP) "You're always late. Just get up and get ready. Everyone else is already dressed."

Kyle and Roger, Pedro's bunkmates, were just about ready to leave to head to the dining hall.

"Wait up for Pedro," Jimmy called to them.

"We're hungry. Why do we have to wait for that loser?" they said. (RIP)

Kyle and Roger waited for Pedro, but once Jimmy was out of sight, they told Pedro he'd have to walk a few steps behind them.

"We don't want anyone to think we're actually your friend, okay?" (RIP)

Once inside the dining hall, Pedro got his tray and was walking over to the table when he tripped over his shoelaces he had forgotten to tie in the rush. He regained his balance, but his milk went flying up into the air and landed in a puddle on the floor.

"Look, it's like a circus act," a kid yelled out, and everyone at his table started to laugh and point at Pedro. (RIP)

"I wonder if he does tricks with balls like those trained seals?" someone else asked. (RIP)

Pedro liked to play sports, but he hated camp because he was the smallest of all the boys. That day, because it had started to rain, they were supposed to play basketball indoors, which was Pedro's very worst sport of all. The counselor asked the players to divide themselves into two teams, the Lions and the Tigers. Within a few minutes, there were 10 boys on each team, with only Pedro and another kid left. (RIP)

The captain of the Lions team said, "We don't want Pedro. He's no good." (RIP)

"He's no Tiger. He's more like a scaredy-cat," said the captain of the Tigers. (RIP) All the other boys laughed. (RIP)

That night after dinner, Pedro volunteered to help some kitchen staff clean up. Two girls saw him sweeping and started teasing him.

"Hey, Cinderella, when you're done, can you come clean our cabins?" (RIP)

Figure 5-2. The Torn Heart story

The Facts of Bullying

- Bullying is something someone says or does with the intent to gain power over or to dominate another person.
- Every seven minutes, a child is bullied on a schoolyard.
- A child is being bullied when he/she is exposed repeatedly to *negative actions* on the part of one ore more other children.
- *Negative actions* can be carried out verbally, physically, and through non-verbal communication, but they are always carried out with the intent to inflict, injure, or discomfort another person.
- Bullying can be carried out by a single person or a group.
- Bullying situations have an imbalance of strength (physical and/or psychological).
- The bully is always in a position of power over the victim(s).
- Direct bullying involves direct open attacks on a victim.
- Indirect bullying involves social isolation and exclusion from a group.
- Studies suggest that one student of every seven are involved in bully/victim problems on more than an occasional basis.
- Studies suggest that bullying decreases as children get older.
- Peers are present in 85 percent of bullying episodes, but they only intervene in 19 percent of these episodes.
- 57 percent of interventions were effective in stopping bullying within 10 seconds
- Children bully to gain power, to be cool, and because of peer pressure, anger, and frustration.
- Bullying can be a learned behavior.
- Bullying crosses social class, gender, and ethnic boundaries.
- Both boys and girls bully. Boys are more likely to use direct bullying, and girls more likely to use indirect bullying.
- Boys carry much of the bullying that girls are subjected to.
- The greater amount of adult supervision, the lower the level of bully/victim problems; 9 out of 10 bullying incidences are not seen by adults.
- Typically, bullying victims are more anxious and insecure than other children; they are often cautious, sensitive, and quiet. Victims suffer from low self-esteem. Male victims are often physically weaker than their peers.
- Bullies are often aggressive toward adults as well as their peers. They generally have a very positive view of themselves, a positive attitude toward violence, and are often characterized by impulsivity and a strong need to dominate.
- Passive bullies are those who participate in bullying, but do not usually take the initiative.
- Bullies are generally popular among their peers.
- Bullies do come in all sizes and can intimidate victims who are physically larger if an imbalance of power exists.
- Bullies lack compassion and empathy for their victim.
- Victims cannot solve bullying problems themselves due to the power imbalance in the bully/victim relationship.
- Children with special needs may be at greater risk of being bullied due to their disability, lack of social integration, or behaviors. Having a disability is not the main reason children are bullied.

Figure 5-3. The Facts of Bullying

Bullying Scenarios

Billy has trouble reading at grade level. Tim, a boy in Billy's cabin, "catches on" and realizes that reading is one of Billy's weaknesses. During a program, Tim repeatedly eggs on Billy to read aloud to the group. Tim's behavior is contagious, and other boys in the cabin begin making fun of Billy and calling him a baby.

Your co-staff decides it would be a great cabin bonding activity to assign each camper a nickname. You also think this could be fun until you realize that the names your co-staff has come up with are derogatory and are making some of the kids feel bad about themselves.

Two of your campers come to you to tell you that other girls in the cabin are constantly leaving them out. Although you haven't seen this behavior first-hand, you do know that these girls are a little more timid and more apt to participate in camp activities while the other girls are more social and don't like to participate in camp activities.

When the session ends, you find out that a group of boys in the unit (who are full-session campers) had been harassing a girl in the unit all session long. They had constantly poked fun at her, calling her "freak" and "weirdo." The girl has already left camp for the summer.

You come back to your cabin in the middle of rest hour and discover your entire cabin group of boys in the bathroom egging on one of the other boys to masturbate in front of them.

After talking to one of the girls in your cabin because you become concerned that she always seems down, you learn that she has been feeling excluded by the other girls in the cabin. She has heard them talking about her behind her back and feels that they never want her to be a part of their conversations.

One of the male campers in the unit has a bad habit of speaking badly about other kids. He has been at camp for many years, and everyone has gotten used to his behavior. This summer, he has decided to pick on one girl in particular who he knows from school, and he constantly calls her "whore" and "slut" both to her face and to others. The other boys in the unit have begun to follow his lead, and the boy she was "dating" at camp dumps her because he starts being made fun of for dating the girl who is "easy."

One of your co-staff is a little timid and not so outgoing. Your campers are very outgoing almost to the point of being inappropriate and obnoxious. Very quickly, you realize that the campers are overpowering your co-staff. They don't like him and walk all over him. It gets to the point where the campers begin bullying this staff member by calling him names, stealing his clothes, and generally tormenting him.

Figure 5-4. Bullying scenarios

Program #18:
Active Duty—Counseling Skill Role-Play

Note: This program can be adapted to any length, with any number of rotations, based on timing and educational needs of the staff.

Goals:
- To give CITs exposure to camper issues that may surface
- To allow CITs to give and receive feedback

Materials:
- Copies of prompts to put on doors (Figure 5-5)
- Tape

Timed Procedure:
0:00 – 0:05　Introduce program
0:05 – 0:25　First rotation
0:25 – 0:45　Second rotation
0:45 – 1:05　Third rotation
1:05 – 1:25　Fourth rotation
1:25 – 1:45　Fifth rotation
1:45 – 2:05　Sixth rotation

DETAILED PROCEDURE

The CITs will break into six groups and will rotate between stations. Each station will take place in a cabin (or other various locations). The CITs will find a prompt that is taped on the door, and pick one person who will role-play the scenario. The other CITs will enter the cabin and sit down. The CIT who is role-playing will knock on the door and enter the situation once his peers have had a chance to seat themselves. The CIT will role-play the situation with the staff person who is already waiting in the cabin. He and the remaining members will debrief the situation after the role-play. The staff member who is the actor is always playing the role of a camper.

Scenario 1: Campers Coming to CIT and Badmouthing Counselors

Prompt: A camper has asked to talk to you after lunch. You know that there has been some animosity between your campers and your co-counselor recently. The campers haven't been listening very well during activities, and in return, your co-counselor has taken away the last three nights of cabin activity.

Actor:
- Tell how much you hate your counselor.
- Tell the CIT you want him to be your counselor, or you want to switch cabins.
- Tell the CIT that you want him to share with the counselor that the counselor is being unfair and ruining your time at camp.

Goals:
- The CIT should have the camper redirect his concern to a unit head, or offer to sit with the kid as the kid talks to a counselor.
- The CIT is a "referral service"—they can listen to the concerns but are not there to solve them. They are there to help the kid make a decision about what to do next.

Scenario 2: Questioning Sexuality

Prompt: Adam asked to talk to you today. He spends most of his time alone and doesn't appear to be "in" with the other kids. He spends more time in arts and crafts and cares more about fashion than the other boys.

Actor:
- He should tell the CIT he feels "different" from the rest of his peers.
- After a few exchanges, he should say he is questioning his sexuality.
- He should say that his peers use a lot of "gay" slang, which alienates him.

Goals:
- The CIT should provide unconditional acceptance.
- The CIT should not push the camper to "come out" to other people or to intervene in cabin dynamics.
- The CIT should listen to the camper, should validate feelings, and see if he wants to be connected to someone else to talk to.

Scenario 3: Bullying

Prompt: Sam is 12 years old and has been to camp before. You have noticed some tension in the cabin between Sam and some of the other boys. He has asked to talk to you about it. You are preparing to go in and ask Sam what is up.

Actor:
- Say you have heard other campers talking about you behind your back.
- Say you feel that they never want you to be a part of their conversations.
- Say that you are bullied by another boy.
- Say that you don't like it here and want to go home.

Goals: Intervening with victims
- Tell the camper that you have noticed that he is upset and want to help.
- Let camper know that if he is being picked on, it isn't his fault.
- Encourage the camper to express how he has felt when others have excluded him.
- Ask the camper to let you know when it happens again.
- One possibility is to have a talk with the cabin about how to treat other people.
- Reassure the camper that his name won't be brought up. As a cabin, have the campers provide input on consequences if this behavior is continued.

Talking point after debriefing role play:
- Intervening with bullies
  - ✓ Describe the behavior that you saw.
  - ✓ Explain and enforce consequences.
  - ✓ Look for opportunities to help bullies develop positive ways of interacting with the victim.
- Cabin strategies
  - ✓ Establish consequences for bullying (talk with staff/unit head or call home).
  - ✓ Be consistent with how you record, report, and prevent bullying.
  - ✓ Pair unpopular children with helpful and friendly children.
  - ✓ Encourage and affirm children when they demonstrate helpful behavior.
  - ✓ Play cooperative games with children.

Scenario 4: Abuse

Prompt: Sally is a 14-year-old camper who has been coming to camp for a long time. In the past she has always enjoyed all camp activities and has always participated. This year, she has seemed slightly withdrawn and has appeared uncomfortable participating in group activities such as campfire.

Actor:
- Should be slightly closed off when asked what is wrong. Deflect questions.
- Make limited eye contact, closed body language.
- Admit she has had a bad year at home.
- Before actor admits what has been happening, say, "Promise you won't tell anyone."
- Her uncle has moved in and drinks a lot.
- Right before camp, she intervened in an argument between her mother and uncle, which resulted in physical violence.

Goals:
- Counselor should thank camper for sharing the information.
- Right when camper begins to share, counselor should tell the camper that that this information will be kept private from peers and will only be shared with people who can help (i.e., director, unit head, or support staff).
- Counselor should listen and make a plan to talk to the unit head together (or counselor will tell the unit head).

Scenario 5: Conversation Boundaries

Prompt: You are walking in to the cabin, and two kids come up who are laughing and in a positive mood. The campers have been talking secretly all day. They have been making some drug references in the cabin.

Actors:
- Actors giggle when counselor enters.
- Actor should say, "He is cool. I bet we can talk to him about it" (or something like that).
- Actor asks counselor, "Do you smoke weed?"
- Actor should say that he has been thinking about smoking recently and doesn't know what to do, but he wants to try it.

Goals:
- Counselors should not answer questions like this, but respond by inquiring about the purpose of the question.
- Counselors should diffuse the conversation and change the direction without alienating the campers.
- Share information with co-counselors and unit head.
- This topic is not appropriate to talk about.

Scenario 6: Homesickness

Prompt: Jon is a 10-year-old boy, and it is his first time at camp. It is the first full day. He came to camp with his two best friends from home. During rest time, Jon is always sitting on his bed alone while his cabinmates are playing cards. The counselor has also noticed that before bed Jon is quiet and retreats to his bed when his friends are chatting about the day.

Actor:
- Wait until counselor asks what is wrong.
- Actor should say that he has been missing his mom and always cries before bed.
- Actor should wait to be consoled until the counselor fulfills one of the goals from the following list.

Goals:
- Creating a structure for camp (explaining how the session goes, how bedtime works, how activities work) will ease the camper's anxiety about what is going to happen.
- The counselor can explore what the camper likes to do and offer to do that activity with the camper.
- The counselor should listen to concerns that camper has without cutting the camper off. If the camper perseveres, then the counselor should cut the camper off.
- Set short-term goals for the camper (e.g., "Let's check tomorrow after breakfast.").
- Don't make any promises about going home or calling.

Prompts to Put on Doors

Include only the prompt part. Do not include the scenario. This will give away the content of the role-play.

Scenario 1: Campers coming to CIT and badmouthing counselors

Prompt: A camper has asked to talk to you after lunch. You know that there has been some animosity between the campers and your co counselors recently. The campers haven't been listening very well during services, and in return, your co-counselors have taken away the last three nights of cabin activity.

Scenario 2: Questioning Sexuality

Prompt: Adam asked to talk to you today. He spends most of his time alone and doesn't appear to be "in" with the other kids.

Scenario 3: Bullying

Prompt: Sam is 12 years old and has been to camp before. You have noticed some tension in the cabin between Sam and some of the other boys. He has asked to talk to you about it. You are preparing to go in and ask Sam what is up.

Scenario 4: Abuse

Prompt: Sally is a 14-year-old camper who has coming to camp for a long time. In the past, she has always enjoyed all camp activities and has always participated. This year, she has seemed slightly withdrawn and has appeared uncomfortable participating in group activities such as camp fire.

Scenario 5: Conversation Boundaries

Prompt: You are walking in to the cabin, and two kids come up who are laughing and in a positive mood. The campers have been talking secretly all day and made some drug references in the cabin.

Scenario 6: Homesickness

Prompt: Jon is a 10-year-old boy, and it is his first time at camp. It is the first full day. He came to camp with his two best friends from home. During rest time, Jon is always sitting on his bed alone while his cabinmates are playing cards. The counselor has also noticed that before bed Jon is quiet and retreats to his bed when his friends are chatting about the day.

Figure 5-5. Prompts to put on doors

Program #19: Why Can't They Just Get Along?

Goals:
- To give CITs a better understanding of what conflict is and how it arises
- To allow the CITs to see the step-by-step process that mediation follows
- To give the CITs the chance to discover their own personal conflict management style and preferred mediation technique

Materials:
- Chart paper
- Markers
- Conflict Management Style Assessment (Figure 5-6)
- Conflict Management Style Assessment Score Guide (Figure 5-7)
- Conflict Management Styles (Figure 5-8)
- Mediation Skills (Figure 5-9)
- Communication Skills (Figure 5-10)
- Steps to a Successful Mediation (Figure 5-11)

Timed Procedure:

0:00 – 0:10	What is conflict?
0:10 – 0:20	Conflict Management Style Assessment
0:20 – 0:25	Conflict management style explanation
0:25 – 0:35	Conflict management activity
0:35 – 0:45	Mediation brainstorm
0:45 – 0:55	Qualities and role of the mediator
0:55 – 1:05	Mediation framework
1:05 – 1:45	Mock mediation
1:45 – 1:50	Wrap-up

DETAILED PROCEDURE

0:00 – 0:10: What Is Conflict?

The CITs will brainstorm ideas on what conflict is and what conflicts are usually about. After a brief explanation of each type, the CITs will come up with examples related to camp for each type of conflict. Facilitator will also go through the four signs that a conflict is escalating.

Conflict: A broad term regarding an interaction between people with differing interests that are perceived as incompatible. Conflict is often inevitable, but constructive outcomes from conflict are frequently possible.

Sources of Conflicts

- Relationship conflict: Strong emotions, stereotypes, poor communication, negative behaviors
- Value conflict: Different ways of thinking or doing, different goals, different ways of life, religion, ideology
- Data conflict: Lack of information, wrong information, different ideas about what information is important and how it should be assessed
- Structural conflict: Destructive patterns of behavior, unequal control of resources, time constraints, set-up of organization
- Interest conflict: Perceived or actual competition over what's important, competing needs

Types of Conflict

- Win/Lose: One person wins while the other loses
- Win/Win: Both people find favor with the outcomes
- Lose/Lose: Neither person benefits from the outcome

0:10 – 0:20: Conflict Management Style Assessment

The facilitator will give each CIT a copy of the Conflict Management Style Assessment (Figure 5-6) and its score guide (Figure 5-7). Each CIT will have the opportunity to complete the test and then score himself accordingly. Once all the scoring is completed, the CITs will be able to determine which conflict strategy they most often use (accommodating, dominant, withdrawing, or passive-aggressive).

0:20 – 0:25: Conflict Management Style Explanation

The facilitator will explain each conflict management style (Figure 5-8). The CITs will then have a more comprehensive idea of which strategy they prefer to use.

0:25 – 0:35: Conflict Management Activity

The CITs will then divide into four groups based on their respective conflict management styles. (If one group has too few or no people in it, ask for some volunteers from other groups to form the fourth group, and consequently the fourth conflict management style). The CITs will have a quick opportunity to familiarize themselves with the description of the behavior associated with their conflict management style. The facilitator will then ask for a volunteer from each group to come forward to deal with a "situation." The facilitator will read the scenario out loud, and each volunteer is to handle the conflict in a manner appropriate for his conflict management style.

Scenarios to Role-Play

- A camper thinks a friend likes his girlfriend/boyfriend.
- A customer is sure that the cashier gave him incorrect change.
- A friend borrowed a sweater and ruined it.

0:35 – 0:45: Mediation Brainstorm

What is mediation? What are the goals of mediation? What are some examples of mediation experiences you have had?

Mediation: With mediation, an intermediary works with parties to help themselves identify and choose an option for resolving the conflict that meets the interests or needs of all of the disputants, *not* someone who acts as judge and makes the decision.

Arbitration: Arbitration, carefully reviewing all of the relevant information, issues a final decision in favor of one of the parties.

0:45 – 0:55: Qualities and Role of the Mediator

The facilitator will explain the different qualities/roles that a mediator plays (Figure 5-9) and will touch upon different communication skills—active listening, summarizing, clarifying, and communication pitfalls (Figure 5-10). The facilitator and the CITs will have a discussion about experiences, and will allow for the CITs to share personal stories of times where they've served as a mediator, or had a conflict mediated by someone else.

0:55 – 1:05: Mediation Framework

The facilitator and the CITs will go through the Steps to a Successful Mediation (Figure 5-11). The facilitator will ask for volunteers to read the information.

1:05 – 1:45: Mock Mediation

The facilitator will ask for three volunteers. Two of the volunteers will be given a scenario and will be acting out a conflict while the third volunteer will attempt to mediate the situation. At any given time, any of the remaining CITs can call "freeze" and either take the spot of the mediator or simply provide a suggestion to help the mediator be successful. The CITs will go through as many scenarios as time permits. After each scenario (time permitting), the group will debrief.

1:45 – 1:50: Wrap-Up

Conflict Management Style Assessment

Following is a list of statements about ways that people relate to each other. Please mark a number between 1 and 4 next to the item depending on how much the statement applies to you.

    4 = This very much applies to me
    3 = This often applies to me
    2 = This sometimes applies to me
    1 = This never applies to me

1. It is really important that my friends like me.
2. When we are doing a group activity, I really like to be right.
3. I would rather ignore a fight that occurred than talk about it.
4. When people bother me, I often vent to other people about it.
5. I have a hard time pushing for my opinion when other people feel strongly.
6. I have strong opinions about how to be a good counselor or how activities should be run.
7. I get nervous when people confront me.
8. I don't tell people when I am angry with them.
9. I would rather let someone be right than get in a fight.
10. I feel okay to argue for something that is important to me.
11. After a confrontation, I like to be alone.
12. I find myself picking at little things that people do.
13. I would be uncomfortable bringing up a conflict with a co-counselor.
14. I have trouble leaving space for other people's ideas.
15. After an argument, I rarely revisit the topic with the person I argued with.
16. If I want my cabin mate to do something like turn off the lights, I usually hint at it rather than saying it directly.
17. I put more importance on preserving a relationship than on sharing my feelings.
18. I am often the decision maker in a group.
19. I don't often tell other people when I am upset.
20. If someone used all of my shampoo, I probably wouldn't say anything.
21. If a friend and I both have a crush on the same person, I will usually take a back seat.
22. I always raise my hand to take leadership roles in programs and activities.
23. I usually don't raise my hand to take leadership roles in programs and activities.
24. I get upset when I don't take a leadership role, but I don't usually raise my hand.

Reference: Johnson, D. (1986). *Reaching Out: Interpersonal Effectiveness and Self-Actualization*. Englewood Cliffs, NJ: Prentice-Hall Publishing.

Figure 5-6. Conflict Management Style Assessment

Conflict Management Style Assessment Score Guide

Directions: Please add up the number of points that you have given yourself on each question. The numbers correspond to the question on the quiz.

Accommodating	Dominating	Withdrawing	Passive-Aggressive
1	2	3	4
5	6	7	8
9	10	11	12
13	14	15	16
17	18	19	20
21	22	23	24
Total	Total	Total	Total

Figure 5-7. Conflict Management Style Assessment Score Guide

Conflict Management Styles

Four styles of managing conflicts can be identified.

Accommodating

People who have an accommodating style put a high importance on minimizing conflict and maintaining relationships. These people will often give and opinion, but won't fight for it if someone else feels strongly about the subject. These people like harmony between others and will often put others in front of their personal goals. When working with someone who has an accommodating style, make sure to ask them their opinion and reassure them that you value their ideas.

Dominating

Those who employ a dominating style put a high value on being right, taking charge, and making sure that their opinion is heard. They are often great leaders, but need to be aware of how their leadership style affects others around them. Sometimes people who dominate are unaware that their style scares others from sharing their opinions. It is important to keep in mind that there is a balance between creating an outstanding product and giving other people a chance to grow. When you are working with someone who has a dominating style, make sure to push to get your thoughts heard.

Withdrawing

People who withdraw are often very uncomfortable with conflict. They are not sure if they are risking a friendship if they speak up for themselves. People who employ this style often don't show others if their feelings are hurt. When you are working with someone who uses this style, make sure to pay attention to their non-verbal cues (e.g., body language and eye contact) to see if they are withdrawing. If they are, take the time to ask them how they are doing and how you can help them.

Passive-Aggressive

People who employ this style value relationships and also value their goals and opinions. These people sometimes get their feelings hurt and then lack the confidence or the language to talk directly to the person who hurt their feelings. Instead of withdrawing from the conflict, they will talk to other people about how they feel, or will act out how they feel without saying it directly. When working with someone who uses this style, ask yourself if they are trying to communicate something with their behavior. Are they acting a certain way because their feelings are hurt?

Figure 5-8. Conflict Management Styles

Mediation Skills

The mediator is:

Unbiased: A mediator is neutral and objective, a person who does not take sides.

An empathic listener: A mediator is skilled at listening with the intent to understand what each person thinks and feels.

Respectful: A mediator is able to treat both parties with respect and understanding, without prejudice.

Helps people work together: A mediator is responsible for the process, not the solutions. When both parties cooperate, they are able to find their own solutions.

Keeps information confidential: A mediator builds the people's confidence and trust in the process by not discussing their problem with others in camp.

Figure 5-9. Mediation Skills

Communication Skills

Communication occurs when a listener hears and understands a speaker's essential thoughts, acts, and feelings. Many conflicts continue because of poor communication between people. In order to communicate, the mediator uses specific communication skills.

Active listening means using *non-verbal behaviors* to show you hear and understand. These non-verbal behaviors include tone of voice, eye contact, facial expressions, posture, and gestures. Lean forward, smile, nod your head, and ignore outside distractions.

Summarizing means you do two things. First, you *restate facts* by repeating the most important points, organizing interests, and discarding extra information. Second, you *reflect feelings* about the conflict. It is very important when summarizing to recognize feelings in the situation.

Clarifying means using *open-ended questions or statements* to get additional information and to make sure you understand. These open-ended questions help keep people talking, while closed questions and statements tend to discourage people from further discussion.

Communication Pitfalls

In addition to using closed questions or statements, the following are some sure-fire ways a mediator can shut down communications:
- Interrupt
- Offer advice/bring up personal experience
- Judge/criticize
- Laugh or ridicule

Figure 5-10. Communication Skills

Steps to a Successful Mediation

1. Open the session.
2. Gather information.
3. Focus on common interests.
4. Create options.
5. Evaluate options and choose a solution.
6. Write the agreement and close.

Step 1: Open the Session

- Make introductions.
  - ✓ Introduce yourself.
  - ✓ Ask each person for his name.
  - ✓ Welcome both parties.
- State the ground rules.
  - ✓ Mediators remain neutral.
  - ✓ Mediation is confidential. (Remember that you cannot promise confidentiality in the case of someone hurting himself or someone else. Always inform the people involved in the mediation of the fact that you may have to report the information to your supervisor.)
  - ✓ Interruptions are not allowed.
  - ✓ Parties must cooperate.
- Get a commitment to follow the ground rules.
  - ✓ Ask both parties, "Do you agree to follow these rules?"

Step 2: Gather Information

1. Ask each person (one at a time) for his side of the story.
2. Listen, summarize, clarify.
3. Repeat the process by asking for additional information.
4. Listen, summarize, clarify.

Step 3: Focus on Common Interests

- Determine the interests of each party by asking one or more of the following questions:
  - ✓ What do you want?
  - ✓ If you were in the other person's shoes, how would you feel? What would you do?
  - ✓ Is (for example) fighting getting you what you want?
  - ✓ What will happen if you do not reach an agreement?
  - ✓ Why has the other party not done what you expect?
- State the common interests by saying something like the following:
  - ✓ Both of you seem to agree that...
  - ✓ It sounds like each of you want...

Figure 5-11. Steps to a Successful Mediation

Step 4: Create Options
- Explain that a brainstorming process will be used to find solutions that satisfy both parties.
- State the rules for brainstorming:
  - ✓ Say any ideas that come to mind.
  - ✓ Do not judge or discuss the ideas.
  - ✓ Come up with as many ideas as possible.
- Help the brainstorming process along by using the following questions:
  - ✓ What could be done to resolve this dispute?
  - ✓ What other possibilities can you think of?
  - ✓ In the future, what could you do differently?
- Write the brainstorming ideas on a piece of paper.

Step 5: Evaluate Options, and Choose a Solution
- Ask for ideas or parts of ideas that seem to have the best possibilities of working.
- Circle these ideas on the paper.
- Evaluate options circled and invent ways to improve the ideas by using one or more of the following questions:
  - ✓ What are the consequences of deciding to do this?
  - ✓ Is this option a fair solution?
  - ✓ Does it address the interests of everyone involved?
  - ✓ Can it be done?
  - ✓ What do you like best about the idea?
  - ✓ How could you make the idea better?
  - ✓ What if one person did _____? Could you do _____?
  - ✓ What are you willing to do?
- When an agreement is reached, check to be sure it is sound by answering the following questions:
  - ✓ Is the agreement effective?
  - ✓ Is the agreement mutually satisfying?
  - ✓ Is the agreement specific?
  - ✓ Is the agreement realistic?
  - ✓ Is the agreement balanced?
- Summarize the agreement.

Step 6: Write the Agreement and Close
1. Write the agreement reached by the parties.
2. Ask each party to sign the agreement, then sign it yourself.
3. Shake hands with each person and congratulate them on working to reach an agreement.
4. Ask them to shake hands.
5. Close by saying, "Thank you for participating in the mediation."

Figure 5-11. Steps to a Successful Mediation (cont.)

Program #20: Conflict Escalation

Goals:
- To learn how to intervene when conflict escalates
- To learn why conflict escalates

Materials:
None

Timed Procedure:
0:00 – 0:10   Conflict escalation role-play
0:10 – 0:30   Discussion about conflict escalation
0:30 – 0:60   Small group role-play

DETAILED PROCEDURE

0:00 – 0:10: Conflict Escalation Role-Play

Conflict Escalation Role Play: Cabin Drama

Scenario: Sara and Sam's cabin just lost their special activity because the bunk was dirty.

Sara: I can't believe that you didn't clean up your bunk. The counselor told all of us that if we didn't clean up our stuff, we wouldn't get to have our special activity later.

Sam: What are you talking about? I did clean up my bunk. That is Erin's camera on the floor. I cleaned everything up.

Sara: No, you didn't. You never clean anything. Like your chore this week is to clean the showers, and you didn't do that. Everyone knows it.

Sam: Well, you didn't do your chore last week of cleaning the windows. That is why our counselor got all mad.

Sara: Mad? She got mad because of something entirely different than that. Every year that we have been in a cabin together, you are always messy, and you always try to date the boy I like.

Sam: I always like them first. Dave liked me, and I liked him.

Sara: No, I said I liked Dave first.

Sam: (shouting) Rachel! Who liked Dave first last year? Me or Sara?

0:10 – 0:30: Discussion About Conflict Escalation

What were the signs that the conflict was escalating?

- More issues are added to the original conflict.
- Issues move from specific to general.
- Number of parties involved grows.
- The party's goals change from "doing well" to "winning" to "hurting the other."

In general, why does this conflict escalate?

- Fear
- Anger
- Negative attitudes
- Stereotypes
- A bid for attention

What should counselors do when a conflict is escalating?

- Tell campers they can only speak for themselves.
- Tell campers that only the current issue at hand is being discussed.
- Give campers a break if they are emotional.
- Do not let campers interrupt each other.

0:30 – 0:60: Small Group Role-Play

Have CITs write down different scenarios that would call for a mediation. Have CITs break into groups of three and rotate through being the mediator. Concentrate on reminding campers to only speak for themselves, redirecting them to the current issue, and making sure they do not interrupt each other.

6

Working With Groups

Philosophy and Basic Concepts

Creating a feeling of belonging is key to creating group cohesion. Group cohesion allows both the CITs and camper to feel safe and comfortable. The process of creating group cohesion requires direction and guidance form the leader. As a counselor, you will be asked to take a group of disparate individuals and mold them into a happy, functioning unit. This process does not happen automatically. It requires direction and guidance from you as the leader of your cabin group. The CIT director and the CITs can help create the feeling of belonging by promoting communication with in the group, taking time to create meaningful one-on-one relationships, and utilizing expected group development patterns.

Basic Concepts

Stages of Group Development

Many different models can be used for group development. This book uses the model of forming, storming, working, and adjourning. This theory can be used to normalize what is happening within the CIT group or can be used as a guide to help design programs for campers. It is also helpful to note that during the storming phase, the group traditionally rebels against its leader (i.e., the CIT director). It is helpful to know that this result is probably going to take place sometime during the summer, and that it is a normal part of group development.

Group Roles

Within the CIT group and within cabin groups, each member plays a different role: social roles, such as the compromiser, group leader, the outsider, the harmonizer, and the advocate. The CIT year is different, because CITs play both social roles, and task roles. Task roles are roles such as the initiator who gives ideas, the elaborator who builds on others' ideas, the evaluator/critic who evaluates the proposals against a predetermined or objective standard, and the supporter who is flexible. The CITs tend to enjoy discussing what social and task roles they play within the CIT group. It is helpful to have them examine what roles their campers play in the cabin.

Process

How group members interact. Did one member talk more than others? Did everyone participate? Did one member encourage others to participate? Look at group roles. Did the facilitator ask and answer all the questions? Did group members challenge each other? (If you were only able to watch the session through a glass window and could not hear anything, what would you see?)

Content

What topic was discussed? Did you stay on track with what you wanted to talk about? Did it bring up emotion in people? Were people closed off or open in discussing these things?

Consensus Building

This concept entails putting unanimous agreement above all other considerations. This skill is important when CITs work together on tasks. The director can come up with a problem or situation in which all of the members of the group must agree on a solution. After this, the facilitator can explore what process the group participated when coming to a final solution.

Program #21: Stages of Group Development

Goals:
- To help CITS learn about the different stages of group development
- To help CITs learn about tasks for the leader that occur at each phase
- To allow CITs to brainstorm techniques related to the stage they are given and then share the information with the other group members

Materials:
- Stages of Group Development (Figure 6-1)

Timed Procedure:
0:00 – 0:10   Introduction to the concept of stages of group development
0:10 – 0:25   Break into small groups
0:25 – 0:40   Share information with the large group

DETAILED PROCEDURE

0:00 – 0:10: Introduction to the Concept of Stages of Group Development

The group leader should create a diagram that shows the stages of group development. The group leader should share the information from Stages of Group Development (Figure 6-1) about what happens during each stage.

0:10 – 0:25: Break Into Small Groups

The large group should break up into four groups. Each group should read about the role of the leader. Each group should complete the activity in their category and prepare to share the information about the role of the leader, and the information they brainstormed related to the activity.

0:25 – 0:40: Share Information With the Large Group

Groups will share their information.

Stages of Group Development

It is important to know the phases of group development, because this will help predict what issues will come up in the cabin and within the CIT group. This information is also great to teach while having CITs develop activities that are relevant to the main tasks of each phase.

Forming

The forming stage is the initial stage in which individuals experience the discomfort inherent in any new situation. Campers will tend to be on their best behavior during this time as they are getting acquainted with you and their peers. Homesickness will arise at this time, and thus, the counselors need to provide a lot of structure. During this time, small subgroups may form, and members discover similarities and differences between each other.

Role of the leader: Individuals want guidance and clear expectations. They want to connect with their leaders to feel safe. It is helpful if they know how the day is structured, what the rules are, and that the counselors are available. It is important to follow through with guidelines that are set. At this stage, it is important to learn different discipline techniques.

Activity: CITs can brainstorm different ways to establish cabin structure and expectations. (In order to create structure, you want to let the kids know what is going on and you want to show them that you are predictable.)

Storming/Transition Phase

Once members are comfortable with the leader and some of their peers, campers may begin to act out to test the leader's authority. The members of the group are set in the roles that they will play in the group and how much power they have. Campers may pressure counselors for more freedom and less rules. It is important to make sure that everyone's voice gets heard and that each member is comfortable in the role he is playing.

Role of the leader: It is very likely that the group will rebel against the leader at this phase. This reaction is totally normal and usually has little to do with the leader's abilities. The leader must listen to camper's concerns, but hold to his expectations and values. Keep lines of communication open and dialogue about conflict that is occurring. Be mindful of bullying that is occurring and intervene early.

Activity: CITs should brainstorm different things that can do if cliques are starting to form. What can a counselor do to break up the cliques? How can they make the camper mix together in a creative way?

Figure 6-1. Stages of Group Development

Working Phase

In this stage, cabins are usually able to function pretty efficiently without much guidance from the leader. Conflict is minimal at this stage, and campers are able to solve their own problems. Cabin members will have taken on roles, which are comfortable to them, and they will be accepting of each other. Close relationships will form, and a group identity will emerge.

Role of the leader: Enjoy the camper's company and help the cabin develop an identity.

Activity: CITs can think of ways they can help the cabin feel a sense of distinctiveness and bond as a group. What physical things can give campers a sense of unity? What else can give a cabin an identity?

Adjourning

Adjourning is the stage when camp comes to an end, and it is time to say goodbye. It is important to process the camp experience and what the campers learned and accomplished.

Role of the leader: The role of the leader is to help campers reflect upon their experience at camp and reinforce positive feelings.

Activity: CITs can brainstorm activities that help provide closure and a recap of the cabin's experience.

Figure 6-1. Stages of Group Development (cont.)

Program #22: Puzzled

Goals:
- To provide CITs with an opportunity to interact with fellows from other programs
- To help CITs strengthen and foster their communication and teamwork skills
- To allow CITs to explore different leadership styles and discuss how to adapt your style to be a part of a team

Materials:
- 50 blindfolds
- 12 copies of the puzzle
- Slips of paper with names on them

Timed Procedure:
0:00 – 0:05   Divide into groups
0:05 – 0:20   Puzzle time
0:20 – 0:40   Group discussion
0:40 – 0:45   Wrap-up

DETAILED PROCEDURE

0:00 – 0:05: Divide Into Groups

As each CIT enters the room, hand them a slip of paper with a name of a famous person on it (for a total of six different groups). If the teens are already in the room, simply pass out pieces of paper. Have the teens divide themselves into the six different groups according to which name they have on their slip of paper. You should have six groups of five people (or whatever is appropriate).

0:05 – 0:20: Puzzle Time

Each group will be given a puzzle and four blindfolds. Each puzzle has the same phrase written on it (e.g., "In a place where there are no humans, strive to be human."). The CITs are not allowed to begin the puzzle until all but one person has put on a blindfold. Once they are blindfolded, the group can begin to put together the puzzle. The activity has a couple of catches: the non-blindfolded person is only allowed to talk when asked questions by the blindfolded people, and can only answer with "Yes" or "No." The non-blindfolded person is not allowed to touch the puzzle. If a team finishes early, switch off the non-blindfolded person, and try the activity again.

0:20 – 0:40: Group Discussion

The groups will reconvene for a large group discussion. The facilitator will engage the CITs in a discussion about the activity in which they just participated, its relevance to the work they do in their camp and the outside world, the quote on the puzzle, and how it relates to both the activity and roles as counselors and leaders.

About the Task

- What were the challenges with this task?
- What was easy about this task?
- Was there a clear leader in the group?
- How did the obvious limitations affect how you worked as a group?
- Can this exercise be related to the work you do in your program? How?

0:40 – 0:45: Wrap-Up

Program #23: Group Dynamics—Meal Time Fun

Goals:
- To learn about group dynamics
- To explore how group dynamics surface at meal time
- To explore possible issues that surface at meal times

Materials:
- One set of camper vignettes per group (Figure 6-2)
- One large piece of butcher paper per group
- One marker per group
- Tape (to hang up butcher paper)
- Dinning hall table (optional)

Timed Procedure:

0:00 – 0:05   Introduce the activity and split into groups
0:05 – 0:25   Activity
0:25 – 0:50   Debrief activity

DETAILED PROCEDURE

0:00 – 0:05: Introduce the Activity and Split Into Groups

Break CITs into groups of six to eight, and give them the 10 camper vignettes outlined in Figure 6-2 that has a description of different campers and counselors. Read the following:

> Your task is to create the optimal environment for dinner. Using the cards provided, decide which campers should sit at which seat around the table. Arrange the 10 names in such a way to set the stage for best interaction possible. As a group, keep in mind how different personality types impact relating styles. When you are done setting the table, please draw a picture of your table and where you have seated everyone.

0:05 – 0:25: Activity

The CITs should decide where each camper and counselor should sit, and then draw where they have seated everyone on the butcher paper. After all the groups are finished, the facilitator should hang up butcher paper side by side so that the different table settings can be compared.

0:25 – 0:50: Debrief Activity

The small groups should become a large group to debrief.

Specific Process Questions

- What are your reflections/reactions?
- How did you come to a consensus?
- What potential problems/challenges did you see that could occur? How did you troubleshoot these issues?
- What values were most important in making decisions? Keeping the counselor happy? Homesick kids? Pushing comfort level?

Application Questions to General Camp Setting

- How to group dynamics play a role at meals/camp in general?
- What is the counselor's role in facilitating group dynamics?
- If a conflict arises, do you put people together or separate them?

Camper Vignettes

Jon: Jon is a young counselor. In general, he is quiet, but he has strong conversation skills when dealing with campers one on one. He tends of get slightly flustered when conflict occurs, but can stand his ground when he needs to.

Jerry: Jerry is the clown of the group and keeps the atmosphere fun. He usually has to be asked twice to stop playing with his food. He made fun of Scott earlier in the day for crying when he missed his mom.

Scott: Scott is a quiet camper. This is his first time away from home, and he is often sad. He tends to sit next to Jon at most meals, and doesn't interact directly with his peers unless they begin the conversation.

Adam: Adam consistently challenges his fellow campers about anything and everything. He makes fun of their shoes and clothes, and thinks he is way too cool for camp. He listens to Max when he tells him what to do, and follows Dan around.

Dan: Dan is cool and collected. He is laid back and goes with the flow. He has not caused conflict, but he has not emerged as a cabin leader, either.

Jarred: This is Jarred's first time away from camp. He also cried a little the first few days, but then stopped once he became close with Dan and Adam. Jarred stopped crying at meals when he started sitting next to Dan and Adam at the table. The three of these campers usually sit next to each other at the table.

Darren: Darren asks questions about anything and everything ("What time is dinner? Lunch?" "Do we have shower hour?"). Max is starting to get a little short with him, which is amusing for the other kids.

Max: Max is the counselor and has a lot of spunk and personality. He is well-liked, although sometimes he has a low tolerance for annoyance.

Blake: Blake is the "perfect" camper. He does everything that he is supposed to, and often seeks positive reinforcement from his counselors. He has sat next to Max the past three meals and asked to sit next to him again. Blake's parents divorced three weeks before camp.

Aaron: Aaron shares the stage with Jerry, but he is not as well-liked by his peers because his jokes are not as funny. Aaron tends to dominate conversation at the table. He has asked to sit next to Max.

Figure 6-2. Camper vignettes

Program #24: Cabin Dynamics

Goals:
- To allow CITs to examine camper traits and interactions in their own cabin using skills learned in Program #23

Materials:
- Paper
- Pen

Timed Procedure:
0:00 – 0:15   Creating a cabin drawing
0:15 – 0:45   Dynamics discussion
0:45 – 0:60   Shifting the dynamics at the table

DETAILED PROCEDURE

0:00 – 0:15 Creating a Cabin Drawing

CITs write the names of their campers around the perimeter of the paper, as well as two or three words to describe that person. The middle of the paper should be left blank. The CITs should then look at how these campers interact with each other and should represent the relationships using the key in Figure 6-3.

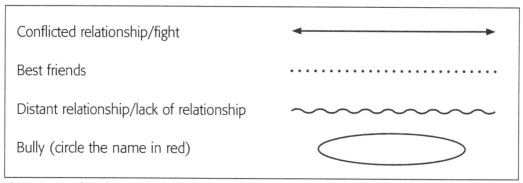

Figure 6-3. Cabin drawing key

0:15 – 0:45: Dynamics Discussion

This discussion is to help the CITs assess the dynamics in their cabin, and discuss ways that they can attempts to shift the dynamics. Possible questions include:
- What do you notice from your drawing?
- What are the qualities that you have written next to the bully, the victim, or the popular kid?

- Does a pattern emerge when comparing the qualities of the bully, victim, or popular kid from different cabins?
- Are there cliques? Individual fighting? Groups fighting?
- What things can you do to shift the dynamics (e.g., include the kid who is left over, intervene with bully, etc.)?

0:45 – 0:60: Shifting the Dynamics at the Table

The CITs should draw a diagram of a table, and pick seats for each camper in the way that would promote the best interaction. (This should be done in the same way that they completed Program #23: Group Dynamics—Meal Time Fun). If possible, CITs should implement the aforementioned seating the following day at a meal and should examine how dynamics have changed/remained the same.

7

Leadership

Philosophy and Basic Concepts

Given that one of the primary goals of a CIT program is to help the teens develop their leadership skills, this broad category can seem daunting and overwhelming. It is general in nature, and that alone can make it intimidating. The key to tackling this vast concept is to keep it simple, and to allow the CITs to develop their own ideas of leadership.

Leadership styles come in all shapes and sizes, and every leader will approach a situation differently. It is vital to allow the CITs to hone in on their strengths as leaders, while providing them with continuous opportunities to develop these strengths within the camp community. A program including an introduction to different leadership styles is a useful tool for counselors-in-training. Many of the CITs participating in your program have had minimal leadership opportunities at home, if any. While you recognize the leadership potential in them, they need to find it within themselves. Each CIT needs to develop his own leadership philosophy—a mission statement or mantra for leadership— to follow throughout his journey as a CIT and future leader in the camp community.

The sample programs in this chapter present leadership from different viewpoints. Some programs present ways for the CITs to explore different leadership styles and develop their own personal philosophy on leadership. Other programs focus on particular skills and theories that fall under the broad category of leadership, including: responsibility, respect, inclusivity, and understanding others.

It is important to focus leadership training on the individual, and how his skills and abilities play a part in the greater team. The purpose of including programs on leadership skills within your grander CIT program is to provide opportunities for the CITs to look at themselves as leaders within the camp community, and their larger home communities. These programs are not meant to stringently define leadership; they are meant to help CITs define, strengthen, and develop their leadership styles, skills, and abilities in a comfortable and encouraging environment.

Program #25: You Can Lead the Way

Goals:
- To assist CITs in understanding not only what leadership is, but also their own leadership style
- To bring the CITs' attention to one of the leadership theories and the different aspects of being a leader
- To draw awareness to the different aspects of the leadership role in which CITs are training to take

Materials:
- Leadership questionnaire
- "A Wish for Leaders" poem (Figure 7-1)
- Five Practices of Exemplary Leadership (Figure 7-2)
- Your Philosophy of Leadership handout (Figure 7-3)
- Chart paper
- Markers
- Lined paper
- Pencils

Timed Procedure:
0:00 – 0:05	Introduction and reading of "A Wish for Leaders" poem
0:05 – 0:10	Fill out the leadership questionnaire
0:10 – 0:20	Brainstorm leadership qualities and definition
0:20 – 0:25	Explain the Five Practices of Exemplary Leadership
0:25 – 0:30	Challenge the process
0:30 – 0:35	Inspire a shared vision
0:35 – 0:40	Enable others to act
0:40 – 0:50	Model the way
0:50 – 0:55	Encourage the heart
0:55 – 1:05	Leadership philosophy
1:05 – 1:10	Wrap-up

DETAILED PROCEDURE

0:00 – 0:05: Introduction and Reading of "A Wish for Leaders" Poem

Explain the concept of the program and relate its importance to the camp setting. The facilitator will read the leadership poem (Figure 7-1) aloud and explain that though being a leader is a tough job, it is one of the most rewarding experiences.

0:05 – 0:10: Fill Out the Leadership Questionnaire

The facilitator should create a leadership questionnaire with the following questions, allowing space under each question for the CITs to write their responses: What is leadership? Why do you want to be a leader? What makes a good leader? The facilitator will give each CIT a copy of the questionnaire and ask them to fill it out, reminding them to keep their answers appropriate, as some of the questions will be addressed to the group later on in the program.

0:10 – 0:20: Brainstorm Leadership Qualities and Definition

The facilitator will lead a brainstorming session, asking two of the questions from the leadership questionnaire: What makes a good leader? What is leadership? The CITs will provide answers to these questions and together come up with a definition of the word leadership. The facilitator will read the dictionary definition aloud, and then work with the CITs to come up with a definition that incorporates what the CITs believe leadership to be, and what the dictionary states that it is. The list of leadership qualities compiled by the CITs will be used again later in the program. (For additional ideas on what makes a leader refer to Figures 7-4 and 7-5.)

0:20 – 0:25: Explain the Five Practices of Exemplary Leadership

Explain to the CITs that many different theories are held about leadership and what it means to be a good leader. Introduce the exemplary practices theory, and give an outline of the five practices (see Figure 7-2).

0:25 – 0:30: Challenge the Process

The facilitator will present information on each of the Five Practices of Exemplary Leadership, and then the CITs will have an opportunity to discuss certain topics that pertain to each practice and will have a chance to relate the information to being a leader in the camp community.

Question: What are some of the ways we challenge the process at camp?

0:30 – 0:35: Inspire a Shared Vision

Question: How can we show our campers that what we're doing at camp is for the good of everyone?

0:35 – 0:40: Enable Others to Act

Question: What are some of the ways we can use the idea of enabling others to act to help our individual cabin staffs?

0:40 – 0:50: Model the Way

This section of the Five Practices of Exemplary Leadership has an activity that goes along with it. The facilitator will ask for a couple of volunteers to share with the group who they consider to be a leader in their lives. It should be someone they know personally, someone with whom they have had contact with in a leadership situation. These volunteers will then be asked to describe a situation in which they had the opportunity to lead someone else, and how they handled that situation. After these experiences, the facilitator will proceed to explain the idea of looking out, looking in, and moving on.

0:50 – 0:55: Encourage the Heart

Question: What are some ways we can recognize our campers?

0:55 – 1:05: Leadership Philosophy

The facilitator will outline what a leadership philosophy is and how it is applicable to being a camp counselor. The CITs will then have an opportunity to create their own leadership philosophies. The CITs will be instructed to answer the questions on the leadership philosophy handouts (Figure 7-3). These answers can then be used as a reference for the CITs during the summer. They can always reread their leadership philosophies and apply them to their placements and other tasks in which they will participate over the course of the summer.

1:05 – 1:10: Wrap-Up

The facilitator will reiterate the importance of the role leadership plays in being a counselor at camp, and the importance in remembering the Five Exemplary Practices in every task.

> ## A Wish for Leaders
>
> I sincerely wish that you will have the experience of
> thinking up a new idea, planning it, organizing it, and following it
> to completion, and then have it be magnificently successful. I also
> hope you'll go through the same process and fail miserably.
>
> I wish you could know how it feels "to run"
> with all your heart and lose—horribly!
>
> I wish that you would achieve some great good for
> mankind but have nobody know it, except for you.
>
> I wish that you could find something so worthwhile that
> you deem it worthy of investing your life in it.
>
> I hope you become so frustrated and challenged enough to being
> to push back the very barriers of your own personal ambitions.
>
> I hope you make a stupid mistake and get caught red-handed
> and are big enough to say those magic words: "I was wrong."
>
> I hope that you give so much of yourself that some days
> you wonder if it is worth the effort.
>
> I wish you a magnificent obsession that will give you
> reason for living and purpose and direction and life.
>
> I wish for you the worst kind of criticism for everything you do, because
> that makes you fight to achieve beyond what you normally would.
>
> I wish for you the experience of leadership.
>
> —Earl Reum

Figure 7-1. A Wish for Leaders

Five Practices of Exemplary Leadership

1. Exemplary leaders *challenge the process.* They are pioneers; they seek out new opportunities and are willing to change the status quo. They innovate, experiment, and explore ways to improve things. Such leaders view mistakes as learning experiences, and they are prepared to meet any challenges that confront them. Challenging the process requires two leader commitments: to search for opportunities and to experiment and take risks.

2. Exemplary leaders *inspire a shared vision.* They look toward and beyond the horizon. They envision the future with a positive and hopeful outlook. Exemplary leaders are expressive; their genuine natures and communication skills attract followers. They show others how mutual interests can be met through commitment to a common purpose. Inspiring a shared vision requires leaders to commit to envisioning the future and enlisting the support of others.

3. Exemplary leaders *enable others to act.* They instill followers with spirit-nurturing relationships based on mutual trust. Exemplary leaders stress collaborative goals. They actively involve others in planning and permit others to make their own decisions. These leaders make sure that their followers feel strong and capable. Enabling others to act requires two leader commitments: to fostering collaboration and strengthening others.

4. Exemplary leaders *model the way.* They are clear about their values and beliefs. Exemplary leaders keep people and projects on course by consistently behaving according to these values and by modeling the behaviors that they expect from others. They plan thoroughly and divide projects into achievable steps, thus creating opportunities for small wins. To model the way requires leaders to commit to setting an example and planning small wins.

5. Exemplary leaders *encourage the heart.* They encourage people to persist in their efforts by recognizing accomplishments and contributions to the organization's vision. They let others know that their efforts are appreciated, and they express pride in their team's accomplishments. Exemplary leaders find ways to celebrate achievements. They nurture team spirit, which enables people to sustain continued efforts. Encouraging the heart requires leaders to be committed to: recognizing contributions and celebrating accomplishments.

Based on *The Leadership Challenge: How to get Extraordinary Things Done in Organization* by J.M. Kouzes and B.Z. Posner. 1989. San Francisco: Jossey-Bass.

Figure 7-2. Five Practices of Exemplary Leadership

Your Philosophy of Leadership

What is a personal philosophy of leadership?

A leadership philosophy is the personal lens through which you see how to behave as a leader. It serves as the moral and ethical compass, which gives direction to your actions.
- Your philosophy continues to evolve over time.
- Leaders use their philosophy in context. Your philosophy relates to the situation in which you are leading.

How do you determine your philosophy?

Developing a working philosophy draws upon what you learn from others and is deepened and personalized by your experience, your value orientation, and your belief system. You must look inside yourself to explore and evaluate your assumptions, attitudes, values, and beliefs about leadership.
- Assumptions are the everyday ideas that you take for granted, but believe to be true. These assumptions are the drive behind taking action. Although you are not aware they exist; they are that on which your expectations are based.
- Attitudes are the opinions that determine the way you think, act, and feel. These guide your behaviors from the way in which you respond to something or someone, to your understanding of the future.
- Values are the innate preferences you have regarding principles and personal standards. These are the moral and ethical foundations, in turn, effecting your communication are displayed in your actions.
- Beliefs are the ideas that form your understanding of reality. You hold them to be true, see them as facts, and they allow you to have confidence in your reality.

How do you develop your own leadership philosophy at camp?

Ask yourself the following:

What are your beliefs and values about human nature?
- Do people influence camp society, or does camp society influence people?
- How do people interact with a community?

Figure 7-3. Your Philosophy of Leadership handout

What is the purpose of leadership?

- How influential is leadership?
- Is it to provide resources?
- Is it to help people change social conditions?
- Is it to make good decisions for people?

What makes a good leader?

- Are there certain qualities a leader must have?
- Is leadership only a value when it helps people solve a problem?
- Who decides who leads?
- How is leadership acquired?
- What are the sources of leader credibility?

What is the leadership process?

- Should leadership always be evaluated in behavioral terms?
- Is leadership a developmental process?
- Does leadership create vision, or does it promote shared vision?
- Are leadership behaviors derived from personal experiences or developed externally?

This information was adapted from Nancy Huber. 1998. *Leading From Within*. Malabar, FL: Krieger Publishing Company.

Figure 7-3. Your Philosophy of Leadership handout (cont.)

What Is a Leader?

A Leader...

- *Believes in himself:* Not conceit or false modesty, but respects himself, sees his own abilities and recognizes them as needed and useful to people and situation around him.
- *Believes in others:* Encourages them to fulfill the potential of their abilities
- *Pursues excellence:* A diligent, single-minded concern for important details, not content with second-rate performance.
- *Admits mistakes:* Realizes his own humanity, and learns from mistakes to move on.
- *Is creative:* Builds on ideas to produce more ideas and considers all sorts of interesting and untested hypotheses.
- *Is a worker:* Often may need to work alone, but willing and able to be fully involved in the group's work.
- *Is a dreamer:* Aware that the mind is full of untapped power, dreaming is the basis for real progress.
- *Is an educator:* Helps others to understand aims and goals and develops their abilities for total achievement.
- *Is a student:* Never ceases learning, doesn't rest on past record, keeps up with new developments, willing to learn from those around him.
- *Is an idealist:* Convinced that people are wonderful, the work is exciting, thinks next year is bound to be better, has a deep-seeded faith in his fellow man.
- *Takes calculated risks:* Is a good guesser, risks to prove hunches, at times lets instinct take priority over natural thought process.

Figure 7-4. What Is a Leader?

10 Qualities of a Leader

1. A leader must be able to take criticism.

No person in a position of authority will be immune from criticism. A leader must learn to sort out the constructive from which he can learn, and the malicious from which he must ignore.

2. A leader must learn to withstand adversity.

Things will not always go well. Failures will happen. A good leader will bounce back.

3. A leader must be able to delegate authority.

He must be able to give up the power, to trust those under him.

4. A leader must make decisions.

The person who cannot take a stand does not deserve to lead others.

5. A leader must be free of prejudice.

It was once said that, "Prejudice is a luxury only little people can afford."

6. A leader must learn to praise others, to share the credit, and to give credit where credit is due.

If he tries to take credit for everything, he will not lead; he will only frustrate those under him.

7. A leader must be able to concentrate under difficult conditions, to keep the goal constantly in mind, to keep his head when all about him are losing theirs.

8. A true leader will assume responsibility for his own mistakes.

9. A leader will not try to avoid responsibility for the mistakes of others.

10. A good leader will grow and learn.

Figure 7-5. 10 Qualities of a Leader

Program #26: It's Just My Style

Goals:
- To help CITs examine different styles of leadership
- To enable CITs to discover the effectiveness and ineffectiveness of different styles of leadership
- To jump start the CITs' own thinking about their leadership skills and styles

Materials:
- Small pack of LEGO bricks
- Three decks of cards
- Chart paper
- Markers
- It's Just My Style leader handout (Figure 7-6)
- Leadership Styles (Figure 7-7)

Timed Procedure:

0:00 – 0:05	Introduction/break into groups
0:05 – 0:15	Rotation #1
0:15 – 0:25	Rotation #2
0:25 – 0:35	Rotation #3
0:35 – 0:55	Discussion
0:55 – 1:05	Leadership Styles
1:05 – 1:10	Wrap-up

DETAILED PROCEDURE

Note: This program will be more effective if the CITs do not know that this is a program about leadership styles. The CITs will get the effect of the program better if they only know that they are supposed to complete a task and do not know they are being subjected to stereotypes of leadership styles.

0:00 – 0:05: Introduction/Break Into Groups

The facilitator will tell the CITs that they are now going to have a non-content based program. They are going to break up into three groups and merely do fun little things in these groups. Once in their groups, the group leader can lead the CITs in a name game or brief mixer.

0:05 – 0:15: Rotation #1

Each group meets with a different leader. The leaders will move from group to group on a rotation cycle and each leader will have a different task and a different leadership style (see Figure 7-6). Each group will meet with all three leaders.

0:15 – 0:25: Rotation #2

Same as Rotation #1

0:25 – 0:35: Rotation #3

Same as Rotation #1

0:35 – 0:55: Discussion

The CITs will come back together as a large group for the discussion. The facilitator will lead the group in a discussion about the different kinds of leadership to which they were subjected. (Hint: Since more than just these three stereotypes exist, each leader's character can be broken down into different aspects of leadership. Discuss all that come up.) If the CITs have not yet realized what the program was about, they will be let in on the big secret at this time.

Discussion Questions

- What kinds of leadership were they subjected to?
- How did the CITs feel when they were just given something to do and then abandoned?
- How would campers feel if they depended on their staff and their staff wasn't available?
- How did they feel when they were given a task to do, and even when trying were put down and berated? Why is it important to maintain a positive attitude with your campers, even in difficult situations?
- How did they feel when they were given a say in what they were doing?
- Which aspects of leadership seem to be more effective?
- Which aspects of leadership seem to make the group less effective in what they were doing?
- Is it sometimes necessary to be rough or strict or mean with campers? Why? When?
- Why shouldn't those traits be associated with camp counselors?
- Why must a leader not try to lead alone?
- Why must a counselor sometimes join the group in doing a task?

0:55 – 1:05: Leadership Styles

The facilitator will go over three different types of leadership styles: autocratic, democratic, and laissez-faire, using Figure 7-7. The CITs will have an opportunity to brainstorm different times and places in camp when these styles are put to use, and will come up with a comprehensive list that can be used for reference throughout the summer.

1:05 – 1:10: Wrap-Up

It's Just My Style

Rotation Schedule

	Rotation 1	Rotation 2	Rotation 3
Group 1	Leader 1	Leader 2	Leader 3
Group 2	Leader 3	Leader 1	Leader 2
Group 3	Leader 2	Leader 3	Leader 1

Leader 1

The first leader leads by showing the group what to do, but then abandons them. The leader distributes small amounts of LEGO pieces to everyone in the group. The leader tells everyone not to touch anything, just to watch the leader. The leader then proceeds to assemble the LEGO pieces, then instructs everyone in their group to assemble their LEGO exactly the same way. The leader should not help the group in any way after the initial instructions. When asked any questions, the leader should just say that the group should know what to do, and that they should be able to do what they need without being "led" further. A possible way to make the group feel abandoned is by talking to the group leader and not letting the rest of the group come talk to them.

Leader 2

The second leader leads by ordering people around. The group has a deck of cards. The leader tells the group that they must build a card tower. The leader should try to instruct the group to build the tower in a very time-consuming manner. When the group goes too slowly or messes up (especially when the cards fall), the leader should berate and scold them. The leader should constantly yell at the group and tell them how bad and dumb the participants are. A good thing to try would be to "accidentally" knock down the cards and then blame it on the group or an individual.

Leader 3

The third leader leads the group by delegating responsibility to others in the group, working by using cooperation and positively encouraging everyone in the group. The leader gives the group a big piece of paper and markers, and tells the group that they need to make a banner that glorifies five different aspects of camp life. The leader should say that they are supposed to include five things, but instead, he feels that the group should think of their own five things (and pretend it's the leader's own idea to go against what the program says). The leader should then let the group break itself up into five groups, each to work on one part.

Figure 7-6. It's Just My Style leader handout

Leadership Styles

Autocratic

- The leader is mostly task-oriented.
- Decisions are made by the leader without group participation.
- Ideas are accepted on the basis of origin (from the leader), not on the basis of merit.
- The autocratic leader is useful in times of emergency or crisis or when time is a factor.

Tell: Okay, it is 10:30 a.m., and it's time for softball. George, get the bat and ball, and the rest of you line up so I can pick teams.

Sell: Hey, it's 10:30 a.m., and I think we should play softball now. We haven't played it for a while, and it's a great game. We'll have fun!

Democratic

- This style is more people-oriented
- The leader's power is granted by the group
- Decisions involve group participation
- Useful in group or committee work

Test: Okay, it's 10:30 a.m. Why don't we play softball if no one has a better idea, okay?

Consult: Okay, it's 10:30 a.m. What do you want to do for the rest of the morning? We could play softball or something else. I would like to get your suggestions.

Join: Okay, it's 10:30 a.m. Let's decide what we're going to do next. We probably all have some good ideas, and if we talk them over, we can come up with something that will please everyone.

Laissez-Faire

- The group has complete freedom to make decisions.
- The leader acts as a resource and contributes only when asked.
- Useful in groups that have worked together for a while.

Delegate: Okay, it's 10:30 a.m. Whatever you want to do, go to it—as long as it's legal. The softball equipment is over there, craft materials are in the box, and the games are on the table.

Figure 7-7. Leadership Styles

Program #27: When I Grow Up—Setting the Example

Goals:
- To gain a better understanding of what it means to be a role model
- To begin to understand the CITs' role as a role model within the community

Materials:
- One empty bingo board for each CIT (Figure 7-8)
- One list of role models for each CIT (Figure 7-9)
- One hat for each group
- Golf pencils
- 25 Bingo chips for each CIT

Timed Procedure:
0:00 – 0:08   Bingo preparation
0:08 – 0:50   Bingo playing
0:50 – 0:60   Wrap-up

DETAILED PROCEDURE

0:00 – 0:08: Bingo Preparation

CITs are split up into smaller group. Each group will be playing their own game of bingo. Each group leader will receive a hat with all possible role model selections for the bingo boards. Each CIT will receive an empty bingo board (Figure 7-8), a list of role models (Figure 7-9), a golf pencil, and bingo chips. The CITs will be asked to fill out their bingo boards by choosing people from the list that they have received that they consider to be role models.

0:08 – 0:50: Bingo Playing

Once the boards are filled out, the fun can begin. Each group will play numerous rounds of bingo. It is up to the group leader to decide the requirements of winning for each round. Once someone in the group has gotten bingo, he must tell the group who was in their winning boxes and explain why he considers these people to be role models in his life.

0:50 – 0:60: Wrap-Up

Wrap-up will focus on a discussion of the purpose and/or necessity of role models in a person's life and where the CITs fit in as role models within the camp community, both this year and in the future years. The program will finish with a reading of the poem "Children Learn What They Live."

Children Learn What They Live

By Dorothy Law Nolte

If children live with criticism, they learn to condemn.
If children live with hostility, they learn to fight.
If children live with fear, they learn to be apprehensive.
If children live with pity, they learn to feel sorry for themselves.
If children live with ridicule, they learn to feel shy.
If children live with jealousy, they learn to feel envy.
If children live with shame, they learn to feel guilty.
If children live with encouragement, they learn confidence.
If children live with tolerance, they learn patience.
If children live with praise, they learn appreciation.
If children live with acceptance, they learn to love.
If children live with approval, they learn it is good to have a goal.
If children live with sharing, they learn generosity.
If children live with honesty, they learn truthfulness.
If children live with fairness, they learn justice.
If children live with kindness and consideration, they learn respect.
If children live with security, they learn faith in themselves and in those about them.
If children live with friendliness, they learn the world is a nice place in which to live.

Bingo

		Free Space		

Figure 7-8. Empty bingo board

Role Models

- Mom
- Dad
- Sister
- Brother
- Aunt
- Uncle
- Cousin
- Grandmother
- Grandfather
- Friend
- Coach
- Teacher
- Guidance counselor
- Camp counselor
- Unit head
- Youth group advisor
- Rabbi
- Priest
- CIT
- Babysitter
- Madonna
- Kobe Bryant
- Rosa Parks
- Abraham Lincoln
- George Bush
- Bill Clinton
- Golda Meir
- Barack Obama
- Michael Jackson
- Oskar Schindler
- Martin Luther King, Jr.
- Anne Frank
- Diana, Princess of Wales
- Helen Keller

Figure 7-9. List of role models

Program #28: Taking Responsibility

Goals:
- To help CITs understand the necessity for taking responsibility for their actions
- To help CITs begin to understand the responsibilities of being a leader

Materials:
- One copy of each scenario for every group (Figure 7-10)
- One copy of each quote (Figure 7-11)

Timed Procedure:
0:00 – 60:00 Scenarios/quotes (9 minutes/each scenario and analysis)

DETAILED PROCEDURE

Participants will break into groups of four or five. Each group will be given six scenarios (Figure 7-10) to act out. Before they begin, one person will explain that when "freeze" is called, everyone must stop what they are doing and listen to the words of the person who is speaking. This person will be reading a quote about leadership and responsibility from Figure 7-11. After the quote is read, everyone will be given a few minutes to ponder the quote before the groups resume from where they left off.

The Scenarios

The group leader will ask the proper number of people to participate in the acting. No person can be involved in the acting more than once until everyone in the group has performed at least once. The group leader will then explain the scenario to these actors, and they have to implement all parts of the scenario through the improvisation. When the acting is over, the group will analyze whether or not responsibility was taken at all, and if it was, where? They will also analyze where it could have been helpful and appreciative had any person in the skit taken more responsibility for the actions that were committed. Each analysis is only complete once the CITs realize how taking responsibility fits in being a good leader.

Scenarios

1. It is the beginning of a sport activity, and the counselor asks one of the campers to please drop off the equipment on the way to their next activity. After the activity is over, everyone disperses and the camper forgets to return the equipment. Later that day, the sports director approaches the counselor and asks where the equipment is. The counselor blames the camper for the missing equipment.

2. You are in desperate need of a radio for your program, and you don't have one. You know that your friend has one and would let you borrow it if you asked. You go to his bunk, but he is not there. You borrow it anyway, figuring that you will bring it back as soon as you are done with it. Your program runs long, and you are unable to bring the radio back right away. An announcement is made at lunch about the missing radio. Your friend tells you that he thinks someone stole it. You are nervous and embarrassed. Instead of telling your friend that you borrowed it without his permission, you tell him that you think it's horrible that someone would do such a thing. The next time that he is out of his cabin, you return the radio. He never know that it was you who had borrowed the radio.

Do Scenarios 3 and 4 together.

3. One of your counselors is supposed to have a program written to be handed in tonight for approval. His co-counselor has approached you and let you know that he has been having trouble coming up with an idea and has nothing prepared. You act as though you know nothing and let the counselor learn a lesson the hard way.

4. One of your counselors is supposed to have a program written to be handed in tonight for approval. His co-counselor has approached you and let you know that he has been having trouble coming up with an idea and has nothing prepared. You come up with a program and tell the counselor about it so that he has something to hand in.

5. Your bunkmates decide to pull a prank. This prank has two different parts; one is very innocent, and the other could get you in a lot of trouble. You decide to participate, but only in half the prank—the innocent half, of course! Only the people who participated in the other half of the prank get caught. You raise your hand and claim that you had nothing to do with it. (Technically, you didn't have anything to do with the part of the prank for which they got caught.)

6. You borrowed your dad's car. While backing out of a parking spot, you lightly tap the car behind you. You figure it's no big deal and don't mention it when you get home. The next day, dad finds the scratch on his back bumper. When he asks you about it, you act like you know nothing. "I mean, someone must have hit you in that stupid parking lot, right?"

Figure 7-10. Taking Responsibility scenarios

Quotes on Leadership

"We create the world in which we live; if that world becomes unfit for human life, it is because we tire of our responsibility."

—Cyril Connolly

"The reason people blame things on the previous generation is that there's only one other choice."

—Doug Larson

"As human beings, we are endowed with freedom of choice, and we cannot shuffle off our responsibility upon the shoulders G[-]d or nature. We must shoulder it ourselves. It is our responsibility."

—Arnold J. Toynbee

"With great power comes great responsibilities."

—Spiderman's Uncle Ben

"Responsibility is the price of greatness."

—Winston Churchill

Figure 7-11. Taking Responsibility—Quotes on Leadership

8

Programming

Philosophy and Basic Concepts

The process of creating programming at camp can be long and frustrating, which is usually due to the amount of time spent on attempting to be creative and innovative and not enough time being spent on process and organization. At many camps, evening programming is an opportunity to do different, fun, deep, emotional, crazy things. This time of the camper's day is 100 percent dictated by the counselors and the kind of experience they want to offer. As a result, much time is spent on ideas and the process can get lost. It is important to process the ideas, but making up your mind and moving forward is as important, if not more.

Getting past the idea stage brings you right into the practical piece of programming. The worst scenario for staff members at camp is when they are rushing around the day of a program to get organized for that evening. This approach can directly affect the way the program itself gets run and will drastically change how the program is received by others. The idea of taking yourself through a detailed process of preparation (as found in this chapter) will inevitably result in a positive experience for you and the program participants.

After you have organized your process, it is essential to organize the flow of the actual program. Making sure that you are keeping proper time and moving your participants smoothly will reinforce all of your previous work. If you put forth your great idea (or topic) in an organized way, but the flow and feel of the actual program is disorganized, then you will bring down the impact of what you were trying to accomplish. You have to make sure all of your staff/helpers understand their roles, and you have to be aware of the time as you move through the program.

Finally, when you are finished cleaning up your program and the dust has cleared, you can sit back and evaluate your program. Evaluate everything from the brainstorm to the clean-up. What did you do well? What could you have done that would have been better? Ask the questions that will push you to be even better the next time. Remember, activities and topics will only goes as far as your organizational process allows you to go. Think through each step, and never be afraid to go over the process until you can confidently stand in front of your program participants and execute your program.

Basic Concepts

Goals: A goal is the aim or ambition of the program.

Objective: The steps that will be taken for someone to reach their goal. The CIT director can emphasize the difference between goals and objectives by having the group play a game like soccer. Tell the CITs to "Go play soccer," without giving any other instructions. After they finish playing, ask them what the goal of playing soccer is. Then, ask them what steps they needed to take to make the goal happen. (Someone will break the group up into teams, each team decided who would play what position, etc.)

Program Vehicle: The structure of the program that embodies the content. (Will the program be run by stations, as a games how, controlled chaos, etc.?)

Materials: What materials are needed to conduct the activity? For CITs to fully understand the process of getting materials, it may be helpful for them to learn the process of requesting materials. Is there a budget? Do they need to ask anyone to sign out equipment?

Timetable: How much time will be given to each part of the activity?

The Path and Process of Wow:
Keys to Writing a Successful Program

Step 1—What Is a Wow Program?

A Wow program is a program that brings out the best in you, your group leaders, and the program CITs. When writing your program, you must set the underlining goal that at least one person walks out of your program saying, "Wow." It's always great to hear people compliment you on a program you have written, but to get the word wow out of someone means you truly wrote a special program.

Where Do You Begin?

It is important in program writing not to repeat history. Doing the same program year after year or simply using someone else's idea is an easy way out. You want to come up with new, innovative ideas for a program or breathe new life into an old idea. A great way to do this is to utilize pop culture. When you are presented with an old idea, see what is popular in the mainstream that your program CITs can relate to. Pop culture also varies with age, so you can in fact do the same topic several times with numerous spins. Another effective way to think outside of the box is to find a topic that, in your personal experience, isn't talked about much in camping or in youth groups. You will most likely find yourself with a topic that the program CITs also haven't had much experience with. This is a great way to create a program that is not only new but can have your program CITs thinking about things they haven't thought of before.

Step 2—The Real Process Begins

Come up with your topic: Something big enough to fit your time frame, but not too broad.

Set a goal: Your goals are the ideas that you want to get across. They create the big picture. You must decide what you want to accomplish.

Objectives: Bridging the gap from topic to goals. Objectives will map out for you how to achieve goals. Objectives are the actual movements of the program itself.

Variables to consider: Keep the following things in mind when creating your objectives and procedure:
- Safety
- Age
- Skill Level
- Time
- Element
- Physical Area
- Facilities
- Climate
- Rules
- Group Size

Step 3—How to Reach Your Goals

Brainstorm: For a set amount of time, all possible ideas are thrown out onto the table. Every idea is a possibility. No evaluation of any ideas should be made during this time, but try to keep ideas limited to the scope of your goals.

Evaluate the brainstorm: Consider all ideas. Do they achieve goals within the time frame you have? Is this idea doable? Does it work for the age group being taught? Don't be afraid to go back or combine several ideas if they work together.

Setting your timetable: After you decide what style you are going to use to create your program, you must set a timetable of what will take place and for how long. It must be flexible, and at the same time you should map out as many details as possible. The timetable also goes into your detailed procedure.

Example: Timetable

0:00 – 0:05	Introduction
0:05 – 0:25	Activity time
0:25 – 0:35	Discussion
0:35 – 0:55	Panel

Activities/Method: What are you doing, and what is going to happen?
- Creative details: What is going to be happening?
- Practical details: Location, supplies, number of group leaders needed, number of groups. Who is setting up?
- Check yourself: Do your activities achieve your goals?
- Age-appropriateness: Physical activities are great for younger children. The more variety, the better. Lots of movement, physical activities, change the location. Older kids can handle more discussion and elaborate tasks.
- Technical details: All logistics should be worked out beforehand.
  - ✓ Who gives intro/who breaks up groups, and how?
  - ✓ Who is the timekeeper?
  - ✓ Who is roaming?
  - ✓ Who gives the wrap-up? What will your wrap-up be?
- Material: Am I ready to go yet? What do I need?
  - ✓ Do they need to be purchased? Collected?
  - ✓ How will they be distributed in groups?
  - ✓ How will clean-up happen?

Wrap-Up/Discussion: Let's get it on: Create a process to get the program participants going on discussing the activity; participants need to "get" what you are trying to teach them. Don't assume they "get it" automatically. You should always allow time at the end to process what happened and if the goals have been met.
- Heavy topics: Keep a small group together as it makes its way through the program. A safe environment will lead to a more open and meaningful discussion.
- Discussion groups: Good questions are *essential*. They should relate directly to the goal concepts and the activities.
- Suggested question formats:
  - ✓ What did we just do/see? Rehash what just happened; it refreshes memories and refocuses participants.
  - ✓ How does it relate to concepts? Gradual progression should be made toward heavier topics.

- ✓ Going around, everyone finishes a sentence similar to the following (This involves all members of the group and gets them thinking.):
  - ⇨ I am doing a good deed when…
  - ⇨ One way I cooperate with people is…
  - ⇨ I think…because…
- The key: Involve as many people as possible.

The Final Step—Review: After the program, take the time to evaluate the program and get feedback. What worked? What didn't work? Did you achieve your goals? Did the participants get the point?

If you follow all of this advice and make use of your most important tool, your mind, you will find yourself on the path to writing a Wow program.

Seven Main Program Vehicles

- Station-Based Program
  - ✓ Carousel: Participants rotate to different stations so that everyone experiences the same things regardless of the order.
  - ✓ Hike through history: Participants visit different stations in a specific order.
  - ✓ Carnival: Participants get to choose which stations they wish to visit.
- Presentation
  - ✓ Skits
  - ✓ Speakers
- Trial/Town Meeting/Debate
- Values Clarification
  - ✓ Four corners exercise: Participants choose one of four options to a series of questions.
  - ✓ Role-playing
- Simulation
  - ✓ Examples: Entering Ellis Island, Wedding, 1970s
- Games
  - ✓ Game show
  - ✓ Giant board games
- Using the Five Senses
  - ✓ Sight
  - ✓ Hearing
  - ✓ Taste
  - ✓ Touch
  - ✓ Smell

Things to Remember

Are you aware of the group dynamics?

- Does the group know each other well?
- Will they respond well to a program that is more discussion-based or activity-based?

Pace, Timing, Location, Set-Up

- How fast or slowly do the programs move?
- Make sure that you allow enough time for introduction and wrap-up.
- Don't rush! You don't want to lose the attention of the participants.
- Don't feel the need to fill time if time remains at the end of the program. People will get bored.
- Be sure to have something else planned in case the program does run short so you don't run into dead time.
- Is the location suitable for your needs? Be sure to structure your environment.

About the Authors

Jessica Furie is a graduate of the George Warren Brown School of Social Work at Washington University in St. Louis, and is currently pursuing her doctorate in clinical psychology at the California School of Professional Psychology. She specializes in conducting therapy with children, adolescents, and families. Furie currently runs the Inclusion Program at Wilshire Boulevard Temple Camps, and has previous served as the CIT director. Furie has presented at the West Coast Summit for Foundation of Jewish Camps. For more information, please email Jessica Furie at JessicaFurie@gmail.com.

Eric Nicastro is an experiential educator who ran the Religious High School program and youth group programs at Larchmont Temple in New York for seven years. He has also spent 10 summers working at URJ Eisner Camp in various roles. Nicastro has recently completed a three-year stint as assistant director at Wilshire Boulevard Temple Camps and the Director of Teen Programs at Wilshire Boulevard Temple. Nicastro is now the Director of Youth and Experiential Education for the Bureau of Jewish Education of Orange County.

Rachel Saslove is a graduate of the Baltimore Hebrew Institute at Towson University, where she earned a Master of Arts in Jewish Education and a Master of Arts in Jewish Communal Service. Saslove has had over a decade of professional experience as an informal Jewish educator, working with adolescents in camp, school, and youth group settings. She worked as a member of the leadership team at Gindling Hilltop Camp and Camp Hess Kramer, and ran the CIT program at URJ Camp George for many summers. In addition, Saslove has worked as a program associate for Hillel of Greater Toronto, and as an educator on the March of the Living. Saslove is currently the assistant director at Camp Mountain Chai, in San Diego, California.